Porcelain in Worcester 1751–1951:
An Illustrated Social History

R.W. Binns FSA

Porcelain in Worcester 1751-1951:

An Illustrated Social History

by
Ray Jones BA

Parkbarn

ISBN 1 898097 00 3

Typeset by Ray Jones in New Baskerville
Originally designed by John Baskerville a Worcestershire man in *circa* 1750
Printed by Severnside Printers Limited,
Upton-upon-Severn, Worcestershire.

Cover: Fine detail from a Chamberlain Inkstand

Contents

Acknowledgements and Author's Note

Some time ago I asked Harry Frost MA, the Curator of the Dyson Perrins Museum, if they had much photographic material concerning the history of Worcester porcelain. I was delighted to learn that there was and so was born the idea of bringing this important historic material to the notice of lovers of Worcester porcelain everywhere. In the six months it has taken to compile and write this book Harry and his Assistant Curator, Wendy Cook BA, have given me endless patient help and co-operation. They are also to be congratulated for their excellent organization of the archive files which has helped me extract necessary information quickly and efficiently.

I would also like to thank Honor Hurley for the use of her new information regarding the Chamberlain family (Honor is a descendant). Thanks also go to all the staff at the Dyson Perrins Museum for their encouragement and enthusiasm.

A number of the photographs in this book originally came from the families of those concerned and we must be grateful for the foresight of their descendants in ensuring that the image as well as the history of famous names is preserved for future generations to enjoy. We have endeavoured to name everyone featured in the following photographs but there are, inevitably, gaps in our knowledge and any help you can give in identifying further people will be gratefully received.

Finally I would like to say that I have so enjoyed researching the background material for this book that I now plan to write a series of detailed histories concerning Worcester porcelain. The first of these will focus on the vital and fascinating First Period and any new information concerning those early pioneering years would be of great interest to me.

Foreword

The amalgam of men and women who have all played a part in the history of porcelain in Worcester creates a fascinating story. People from all walks of life, including doctors, clergymen, and bankers, as well as the more obvious callings, have all been employed within its portals. Whatever their contribution they have always worked as a family through succeeding generations and this has been their strength.

The world of Worcester porcelain would not exist without these people and this volume concerns itself essentially with the evolution of the Worcester porcelain factories and the workforces that inhabited them. Ray Jones takes us on an absorbing journey charting the history of the various factory sites at Warmstry House, Diglis, Saint Martin's Gate and Shrub Hill.

Wendy Cook, my assistant, and I applaud the author on creating this unique volume from the archives we have at our disposal at the Dyson Perrins Museum. We are grateful that at last some of the work we have done in the major re-organization of the archives over the last ten years is now coming to fruition in this way.

This volume is an essential addition to the library of any person remotely interested in the evolution of porcelain in Worcester. It is a story of human endeavour and of people who have devoted their working lives to the potter's art in Worcester.

Harry Frost MA
Curator of the Dyson Perrins Museum

Introduction

'A philosopher seeking among the products of human industry the one which would best enable him to follow through the course of ages, the progress of intelligence, and give him the approximate measure of the artistic tendencies of men, would select incontestibly the works of the potter. Clay from its plastic nature lends itself to the idea of modelling, and gives scope alike to the liveliest flights of imagination and the more persevering efforts of industry. Abundant in its variety, easily procured, and consequently devoid of intrinsic worth, it derives its value solely from the elegance of form imposed upon it by the potter, or from the richness of decoration given to it by the artist.'

The above remarks were made by Jacquemart and quoted by R.W. Binns in his important early book *Worcester Pottery and Porcelain 1751-1851*. The fact that porcelain has now been made in Worcester for well over 200 years gives the city a most fortunate aspect to its industrial and social history. The highs and lows, the successes and failures of the antecedents of the present company have been the subject of continuous research and comment.

Most of the works published on the history of Worcester Porcelain concentrate on the superb wares produced by the different factories. This book is focussed on the development of the industry in Worcester, the personalitics behind that development, and the workers who made the hopes and dreams of ambitious entrepreneurs a reality. No attempt, however, has been made to write a chronological history as this would require a far longer and more detailed publication. Emphasis has therefore been placed on the superb photographs, engravings and ephemera contained within the archives of the Dyson Perrins Museum.

The reasons for the establishment of porcelain manufacture in Worcester are still not totally clear and several possibilities can be put forward for its raison d'être:-

a) R.W.Binns alludes to the politcal motives whereby the establishment of a porcelain manufactory would enhance the strength of the Whig party in Worcester (Dr. Wall was known to be staunchly loyal to the Hanoverian dynasty).

b) Dr. Wall and William Davis had been conducting experiments in Broad Street, Worcester and had evolved a new process of making porcelain. The natural progression from this would have been the formation of a local manufactory. Furthermore there had been a considerable decline in the cloth trade and new industry was desperately needed in Worcester.

c) Worcester was an important city. Although not as important as in the seventeenth century when being one of the ten largest places in the country it was still a city of tremendous influence, economically and politically.

d) Although not close to the source of raw materials Worcester lay astride the navigable river Severn and therefore heavy and bulky raw materials could readily be transported to the chosen site.

The political aspect appears to be the strongest influence in many respects for the original Worcester proprietors were to purchase the Bristol manufactory of Benjamin Lund and William Miller in February 1752 and apparently moved all the stock, moulds and utensils to Worcester.Bearing in mind that Bristol was one of the principal cities and ports in the country and that the soapy rock, so vital to the manufacturing process, was sourced in Cornwall to move a manufactory 'lock, stock, and barrel' to Worcester suggests that more than straight economics were involved.

The Warmstry Site 1751-1840

The site in Worcester chosen for the manufacture of porcelain may appear to be strange to us today but on close examination it was certainly, in contemporary terms, an ideal site. For Warmstry House was a historic property and hardly a likely site for a factory but its extensive gardens lying adjacent to the River Severn were suitable for the storage of raw materials transported on water and, furthermore, the main buildings were suitable for adaptation into the various workrooms required. The lease for the property was signed on the 16th May 1751 and was granted by William Evett, a glover, to Richard Holdship the younger, also a glover, for a term of 21 years, but renewable for 21 years more on payment of a £20 fine, at the yearly rate of £30 per annum. How long it actually took to transform this property into a fully functional manufactory is a matter of conjecture but a period of several months must have been involved. The first definite proof we have of goods being offered for sale appeared in an advertisement accompanying the earliest known depiction of the manufactory in the *Gentleman's Magazine* of July 1752: 'A sale of this manufacture will begin at the Worcester music meeting on September 20 with great variety of ware, & tis' said at moderate price.'

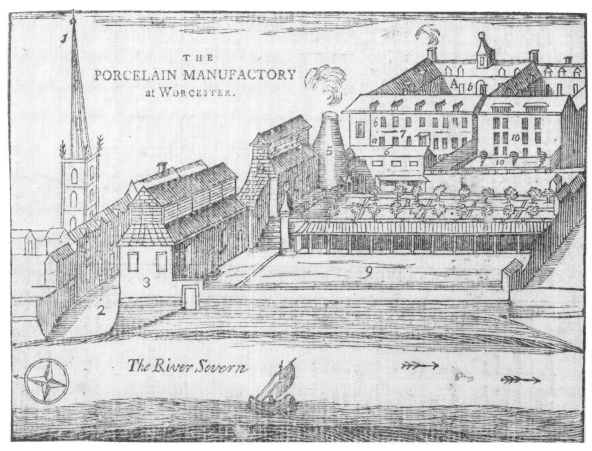

1 The Porcelain Manufactory at Worcester in 1752.

1. St. Andrew's Church 2. Warmstry Slip 3. Biscuit Kilns 4. Glazing Kilns 5. Great Kiln for seggars [sic] 6. Pressing and Modelling Gallery on the first floor (a) 7. Rooms for throwing and turning and stove-drying the ware; on the second floor (b) the eight windows in two large chambers in which the ware is placed on stillions; the same on the east and north where are the painters rooms. 8. The garden. 9. The yard for coal. 10. The house and garden of Mr. Evett, the landlord. The beginning of the process on the ground floor was carried on under the quadrangular buildings marked A; in the north west angle was the great roller and ring; in the north-east the the horses turned the same and the levigators near the roller. The next on the same ground floor was the slip and treading rooms; behind 4. was the glazing room, and behind 5. the secret room.

1

The original partnership deeds of the *Worcester Tonquin Manufacture* are dated the 4th of June 1751 and proudly preserved in the Dyson Perrins Museum. They reveal considerable information about the company. Doctor John Wall and William Davis are accredited with the invention of a new manufacture of Earthen Ware and are rewarded with the effective assignation of free shares. Thirteen other partners are listed and, significantly, one of these is the proprietor of the *Gentleman's Magazine* - Edward Cave - which helps to explain the interest of that publication in a new industrial venture! Cave was a successful printer and publisher and there is little doubt that he was well acquainted with many of the literary and scientific characters of the time. Included among these would have been Doctor Wall for whom Cave had published various medical articles.

Another partner of great significance was the entrepreneurial Quaker Richard Holdship who negotiated the lease of Warmstry House and also the purchase of Benjamin Lund's Bristol manufactory in 1752 (Lund was also a Quaker). Holdship had raised a considerable sum of money by persuading his wife to sell off her Somerset estates and this also enabled him to personally buy the lease of a soaprock mine at Kinance in Cornwall. This was the source of Lund's soaprock and Richard Holdship reached agreement with the other partners to supply them with this soaprock at an agreed minimum quantity of 20 tons per year at a price of £18 per ton for a term of 20 years. Further evidence of Richard Holdship's aspirations are shown by his purchase of three small tenements adjacent to Warmstry House which he demolished and then built a magnificent new house as shown on page 3. Of the other partners several are thought or known to be Quakers. Among these were Josiah Holdship (Richard Holdship's older brother), John Thorneloe (a devout Quaker), William Davis, and Edward Cave. Other partners included William Baylies (a physician of Evesham and along with Cave the major subscriber - both contributed £675 10/-), Samuel Bradley (a goldsmith of Worcester who was to sell the wares in his High Street shop), and Richard Brodribb who was the treasurer for the new company.

2 Doctor John Wall (1708-1776).

3 Edward Cave (1691-1754).

4 A West Prospect of the Worcester Porcelain Manufactory with Mr. Holdship's new buildings.

Robert Hancock made the above engraving in 1757. The buildings to the left of the sail are those of the Worcester Porcelain Manufactory and can be clearly related to the engraving used in the *Gentleman's Magazine* (fig 1). In the interests of artistry, however, Hancock has failed to depict landlord Evett's house (the fine detail of the sail would have been obscured by a house in the background) and this illustrates the dangers of accepting old engravings at face value. Richard Holdship's new buildings certainly look majestic and it is interesting to note that Hancock himself resided in these buildings during his later years at Worcester.

Hancock is thought to have come to Worcester from Battersea around 1756 but there is a school of thought that he may have done transfer printing at Bow beforehand. Beyond doubt, however, is the fact that Hancock was a master engraver and an immensely influential employee. The transfer printing at Worcester was of the highest quality and Hancock must have been well rewarded for his endeavours. Indeed he eventually became a partner of the concern being one of six partners in 1772. Hancock left Worcester for pastures new in 1774 after disagreements with the other partners. Two famous pupils of Hancock were Valentine Green and James Ross. Both were engravers of considerable note while Green is also well known for his early topographical histories of the City of Worcester.

The 1770s saw a decline in the financial fortunes of the Worcester manufactory and this was partly due to the fact that the remaining original partners were ageing and perhaps inevitably losing their enthusiasm and thrust. Therefore it was not surprising when the London agent of the company, Thomas Flight (1726-1800), bought out the old proprietors in 1783.

5 Robert Hancock (1730-1817).

6 John Flight (1766-1791).

7 The diary of John Flight.

Flight only had to pay £3,000 for the company which makes an interesting comparison with the valuation of Robert Hancock's one sixth share in 1774 of £900 (giving a valuation of the company of £5,400). Little is known of the initial years of the Flight period but we are indebted to one of Thomas Flight's sons, John, for considerable information about the company during the years 1788 - 1791. John kept an extremely detailed diary during that time and thus we have been able to gain an insight into the running of a porcelain manufactory in the late eighteenth century. Life in the factory was far from easy at this time: sulphur was ruining much of the ware in the kiln and the chief manufacturing clerk was less than co-operative in helping to solve the problem. Serious consideration was even given to moving the factory to Wales where coals were cheaper. King George III's visit to Worcester in 1788, however, helped to transform the fortunes of the beleaguered company. Flight's diary reveals that this visit was somewhat fortuitious (the King was at Worcester because of

8 Engraving by Hancock.

the music meeting of the three choirs of Worcester, Hereford and Gloucester and was staying at the Bishops Palace): 'The King being of a Curious Mechanical Turn and fond of seeing manufactories of all sorts we hoped he might visit ours but it was a matter of so much uncertainty that I did not like to mention my hopes for fear of a disappointment'. But the King did duly visit their newly opened shop at 45 High Street and Flight's invitation to visit the manufactory itself was taken up the following day. The King and his party spent over two hours viewing the manufactory and left ten guineas with the proprietors for the workmen. The King was very impressed by the Worcester wares and ordered porcelain for himself but, more importantly, he awarded the company it's first Royal Warrant. He also advised the company to open a new showroom in London and this advice was taken most seriously (any thoughts of moving to Wales were now abandoned). Terms were speedily agreed for the rental of No. 1 Coventry Street in the Haymarket and this proved to be a good outlet for the wares of the company. Indeed Valentine Green commented in 1795 that the establishment was most liberally honoured by different branches of the royal family, and also the principal nobility and gentry of the kingdom. The unfortunate John Flight, however, did not benefit from the changing fortunes of the company as he died at the early age of 25 in July 1791.

9 London showrooms at Coventry Street.

Following the death of John Flight a new partner was sought and this turned out to be Martin Barr of Worcester - a local businessman. A rather strange tale exists of how Barr obtained the necessary finance to buy into the company. This tale was related to R.W. Binns by James Knight of Worcester in 1877:

'He (Barr) was putting up the shutters of his not pretentious shop one evening after dark, when a drunken dragoon officer picked a quarrel with him. From words they came to blows, and the soldier cut Barr severely over the head with his sword. The publication of the business would have led perhaps to his being cashiered - certainly to very unpleasant consequences; so he hastened on becoming sober and conscious of the gravity of the mischief he had done to make pecuniary compensation and stop Barr's mouth. A large sum - for those days - was handed over, and with the money, thus acquired, in satisfaction for his cut head Barr became a partner in the china works. The late

10 Martin Barr (1757-1813).

11 The Royal China Manufactory 1795 (drawn and engraved by James Ross).

Robert Gillam, so long in practice as a solicitor here, was a son of the Gillam with whom Barr was in partnership in Lich Street. It was commonly said that Barr had made his fortune by his enlivened scence [sic].'

Whether this story is true or not can never be verified by it's very nature but what is for sure is that Barr was to prove an invaluable addition to the now reviving company.

The fine engraving on the opposite page depicts the Warmstry factory during the Flight and Barr period. It was first published in the excellent *History And Antiquities Of The City And Suburbs Of Worcester* written by Valentine Green. This was drawn and engraved by James Ross who continued to have a close connection with the company as revealed by his Account Books which still exist today. A note of Martin Barr's death occurs in these Account Books: 'Mr. Barr died of Appoplexy, Nov. 10th 1813 in his 57th year, and was buried at the Angel Street Chapel (north and south) on the 18th following. J.R.'

George Barr now became a partner in the company joining Joseph Flight and Martin Barr Junior (George's older brother had become a partner in 1804). These three partners were to remain together until Joseph Flight's death in 1838 and his death was the beginning of the end of the Warmstry manufactory. Negotiations with the local rival company - Chamberlain's - were soon started and it is apparent that the two Barrs were not greatly interested in continuing in porcelain manufacture on a day-to-day basis. However they were still to have a financial interest in the new company which was to be centred on the present Diglis site. The Warmstry site was put up for sale but was not sold off immediately and tiles were manufactured there for a few years.

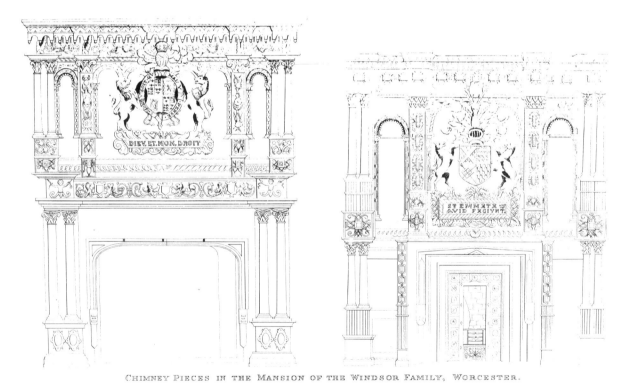

CHIMNEY PIECES IN THE MANSION OF THE WINDSOR FAMILY, WORCESTER.

12 Chimney pieces in the rooms of the Warmstry Manufactory.

Even as late as 1837 parts of the Warmstry manufactory still showed evidence of it's illustrious past. The *Gentleman's Magazine* of May 1837 showed the details of these two elaborately ornamental chimney pieces that were to be found in two of the rooms on the first floor. They dated back to the time of James I. The article accompanying the illustrations also mentioned other carvings to be found in the building and it is interesting to note that one of these depicted crescents of similarity to the famous crescent mark of early Worcester porcelain.

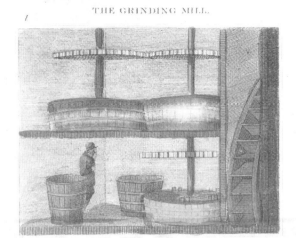

THE GRINDING MILL.

THE SLIP KILNS.

TEMPERING THE CLAY.

FORMING ON THE WHEEL.

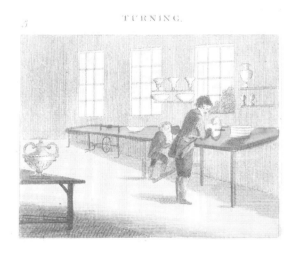

TURNING.

MODELLING.

13 Process of the manufacture of porcelain, in the Royal China Works, Worcester.

An illustrated booklet was published in 1810 detailing the process of porcelain manufacture at the Warmstry site. This was also published as a series of educational cards for children and even as a jigsaw puzzle. The only known surviving example of this jigsaw puzzle is now on display in the Dyson Perrins Museum. The booklet gives a clear and concise explanation of the processes involved and, furthermore, informs us that this was the same process of manufactory as shown to King George III and Queen Charlotte on the occasion of their visit to the City of Worcester in 1788. The booklet is reproduced in full in Henry Rissik Marshall's book *Coloured Worcester Porcelain of the First Period* (1954).

THE BISCUIT KILN.

DIPPING OR GLAZING.

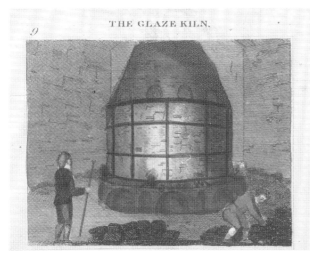

THE GLAZE KILN.

PAINTING.

ENAMELLING KILN.

BURNISHING.

Two other contemporary accounts of interest are those of Valentine Green in *A Survey of the City of Worcester* published in 1764 (reprinted in full in Dr F. Severne Mackenna's *Worcester Porcelain* 1950, pages 48 to 50), and the letter of Mrs. P. Lybbe Powis written the day after she visited the Worcester manufactory on 28 August 1771 (also reprinted in *Worcester Porcelain*, page 55). Her letter is particularly interesting in that it mentions that about160 persons are employed of whom many are little boys and also she discusses the process of making figures in the seventh room. For many years some collectors doubted the existence of eighteenth century Worcester figures but examples have now been identified although specimens are exceedingly rare and very highly valued.

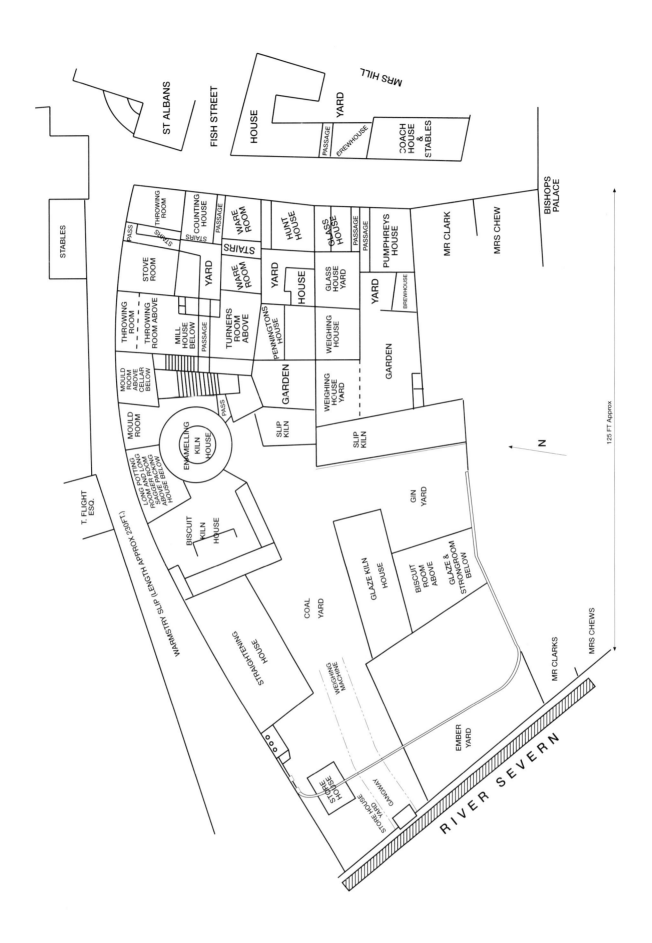

14 Plan of the Warmstry factory adapted from the map drawn by George Young in 1793. Many of the rooms were let off at different times and even employees themselves were known to live on the premises and the Pennington referred to on the plan is probably the renowned painter, John Pennington.

The Diglis Site 1783 - 1851

15 Chamberlain's porcelain works from the Bath Road around 1820.

The manufacture of porcelain on the Diglis site owes it's origins directly to the Warmstry manufactory. This is because the founder of Chamberlain's - Robert Chamberlain - was reputed to be the first apprentice employed by the Worcester Tonquin Manufacture in 1751. There was a long held tradition in the Chamberlain family that Doctor Wall had brought Robert and other members of his family up from the Chelsea factory but this has since been proved to be a fallacy. Robert was actually born in Worcester in 1736 and evidence suggests that the family was of fairly humble origins as, for a number of years, Robert was receiving parish relief payments. Robert soon became an important employee at the Warmstry manufactory and Valentine Green notes in 1796: 'The ornamental part of the productions of that factory, and the embellishing of the ware, were carried on under the immediate direction of Mr. Chamberlain and his son for many years'.

Unfortunately there is no conclusive evidence concerning Robert Chamberlain's actual career progression. We do not know if Robert's split with his employers was amicable: he may have become an independent decorator with, or without, their agreement and they could even have been his biggest customer for sometime. However at some stage, Robert must have decided to manufacture porcelain in his own right and plans to do this could have been formulated some years before production started in earnest. Valentine Green gives the establishment date as 1788 and it is highly likely that this was the date when the first porcelain was produced. It is interesting to note that Chamberlain's opened their own retail outlet in the High Street in June 1789 and this is further evidence that they were then manufacturing on a full scale basis (Flight writes on the 28th June 'Yesterday Chamberlain opened his shop. I was rather surprised as I thought they were hardly ready yet but they talk of making a flaming show in about two months').

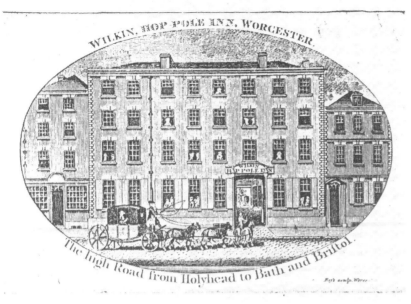

16 *A rare engraving of the Hop-pole Inn.*

The fully functional Chamberlain's manufactory made rapid progress and Valentine Green commented in 1796: 'This work, although in an infant state, is in rapid progress towards perfection; it has already been honoured with commissions from their Royal Highnesses the Prince of Wales and the Duke of York, for whom have been completed two very superb services of their ware, ornamented in a very masterly and elegant style.'

In August 1802 Chamberlain's received a considerable boost to their prestige when Admiral Lord Nelson chose to visit their factory and shop rather than the rival Flight and Barr. This could have been due to the fact that Nelson stayed at the Hoppole Inn while in Worcester and the proprietor was a friend of the Chamberlain's. James Plant - an employee - described Nelson's entry to the painting shop as follows: 'a very battered looking gentleman made his appearance (he had lost an eye and an arm), leaning on his left and only arm was the beautiful Lady Hamilton, evidently pleased at the interest excited by her companion; and then, amongst the general company following after, came a very infirm old gentleman - this was Sir William Hamilton.'

17 *Portrait medallion of Admiral Lord Nelson.*

The portrait medallion of Nelson in fig. 17 is a superb piece of craftsmanship consisting of a finely modelled portrait in bisque set in a gilt surround with a glazed border stunningly decorated with raised jewellery in red, yellow, green and purple encircled by white pearls on an underglaze blue ground. This is most probably the work of Thomas Baxter (reverse is inscribed TB) when he was at Worcester between 1815 and 1821. Baxter is regarded as one of the finest English porcelain decorators and was described by Solomon Cole (a great Flight and Barr painter) as follows: 'Thomas Baxter may be said to stand unrivalled in this country as a classical figure painter on porcelain. He had one advantage over others, that of being a student of the Royal Academy for some years, and was esteemed one of the best draughtsmen of his time.'

18 *Thomas Baxter (1782-1821).*

19 Humphrey Chamberlain (1762-1841).   *20 Mr & Mrs Walter Chamberlain.*

Robert Chamberlain had died in 1798 after a lingering illness but his sons were more than able to build on the foundations laid down for them. Both Robert Chamberlain junior (1755-1832) and Humphrey Chamberlain were partners in the concern by 1796. Humphrey appears to have been the most prominent partner and he was ably assisted by his wife Ann in the day-to-day activities of the company. Their efforts were further rewarded by the award of the Royal Warrant in August 1807. Robert and Humphrey were also involved in the civic life of Worcester and both of them had the distinction of serving as Mayor of Worcester during their lives.

Humphrey had two sons who were to be important members of the company. Best known of these is Humphrey junior whose quality of painting on porcelain is similar in standard to that of Thomas Baxter. Indeed Laird wrote in 1810: 'Some of his works, on a service for the Prince Regent, being copies from historical engravings of English History, are quite exquisite both in the outline and brilliancy of the colouring.' Being the proprietor's son Humphrey was allowed to sign some of his work which was quite unusual in the early nineteenth century. Unfortunately Humphrey junior died at the early age of 33 in 1824. His brother Walter also painted on porcelain in the 1810-20 period but he later became more concerned with the day-to-day management of the company. Walter was to remain a proprietor of the company right up until the Kerr and Binns period.

Chamberlain's appeared to prosper more than their great rivals at the Warmstry site and in 1840 they effectively took over the original company and production became centred on the Diglis site. Mr. R. W. Binns called this 'a Marriage of Convenience and not of love' and one senses that the amalgamation represented a general decline in both firms fortunes. There was also a reduced production of quality wares during the 1840s and it was not until the arrival of two Irishmen - W.H. Kerr and R.W. Binns - that matters were to change greatly.

WORCESTER'S GREAT STORM-MAY 27TH 1811 (extract from a local newspaper).

'A visitation of a singularly awful and destructive nature befel this city and environs between four and five o'clock p.m., when clouds of a horrible blackness came up from the S.E. accompanied by a hideous noise. Shortly hail began to fall, which almost immediately became a storm of ice, and fell furiously in flakes of about five or six inches in circumference. The windows of almost every house which faced the S.E. were wholly demolished in a few minutes. Gardens were laid utterly waste; and fields, both of grass and corn, sustained irreparable injury. The ice storm was succeeded by heavy torrents of rain, with all the terrors of a tropical tempest. The river Severn in one hour rose six feet, and continued gradually to swell its torrent till it had reached the height of twenty feet; and the flood, rapid and wide spreading, swept away in its impetuous career whole herds of cattle from the adjacent fields. 1200 panes of glass were broken in Messrs. Barr's china factory, 500 in the workhouse, and 2000 in Messrs. Chamberlain's factory.'

A further 102 panes were broken at Barr's High Street shop and Mr. Barr commented that: 'Orders will be delayed by the event, but we will do our best.'

RULES AND REGULATIONS

TO BE OBSERVED BY ALL

PERSONS EMPLOYED IN THIS MANUFACTORY.

TIME.

1.

All Persons employed in this Factory to assemble at **HALF-PAST SIX O'CLOCK** throughout the year.

2.

BREAKFAST TIME, HALF-PAST EIGHT to **NINE.**

3.

DINNER HOUR, ONE to **TWO, P.M.**

4.

Every day's work reckoned to terminate at **SIX, P.M.**

5.

All work not ready to be passed through the Warehouse by **SIX O'CLOCK, P.M.,** on Friday, not reckoned for until the week following.

6.

Half an Hour allowed for assembling in a Morning, after which the Entrance Door will be locked; and a **Quarter of an Hour** at Breakfast and Dinner (except to day men.)

7.

On Saturdays, Manufacturing labour to cease at **FOUR, P.M.,** from which time to hour for paying Wages, hands to employ themselves in cleaning rooms and benches, putting tools, &c., in order throughout the Works.

8.

Wages commence paying at **FIVE O'CLOCK, P.M.,** on Saturdays throughout the year.

CONDUCT.

1.

SWEARING and **BAD LANGUAGE** strictly forbidden at all times.

2.

During work hours **SILENCE** and **ORDER** are required, and at all time steadiness and propriety of conduct recommended.

3.

SOBRIETY, CIVILITY, and **PUNCTUALITY,** are indispensable for length of service.

4.

Useful reading at proper times approved. All immoral Publications and Prints found in the Works **DESTROYED,** and their Owners **DISCHARGED.**

5.

"**ON NO PRETENCE WHATEVER**" is intoxicating drink, of any description, allowed in the **Works,** and smoking is strictly prohibited.

6.

Such of the hands as take meals on the premises, are required to do so in their respective workshops, or in the case of Girls in the room appropriated to their exclusive use.

7.

Any Person found loitering in another **Working Room** will be fined unless he can give satisfactory reasons.

8.

Boys are not allowed to play on the **Premises.**

CHAMBERLAIN AND CO.,

Royal Porcelain Works, Worcester.

MARCH 1st. 1851.

21 Notice displaying rules and regulations to be observed by all employees - March 1st, 1851.

Kerr and Binns 1851-1862

22 W.H. Kerr (1823-1879).

23 Kerr vase.

W.H. Kerr of Dublin had been connected to the Chamberlain family by marriage and as a result entered into partnership with Walter Chamberlain and Frederick Lilley in 1850. His two partners, however, were soon to retire and in 1851 he invited R.W. Binns to join him and so started the partnership that was to revive the fortunes of a now ailing business. Kerr was particularly instrumental in repairing old and worn out buildings and planning further improvements such as a new mill, new ovens and workshops. Many more models and figures were made using a new type of porcelain called parian. Kerr decided to return to Ireland in 1862 and was presented with a valuable vase by the workpeople of the Royal Porcelain Works as a token of their affectionate remembrance and regard. The vase was porcelain having a fine cobalt-blue ground upon which were painted subjects in the style of the Limoges enamels. The principal subject was designed from Homer's hymn called 'The Furnace' and represented Homer singing to the potters of Samos, who, in return, present him with some of their vases. On the neck of the vase, also painted in enamel, were portraits of Mr. and Mrs. Kerr which were, apparently, 'remarkable for their fidelity of expression'.

It should be noted that the Company was never actually called Kerr and Binns between 1851-62: W. H. Kerr and Company was the trading name until the joint stock company was formed in June 1862.

24 William Boyton Kirk (1824-1900).   *25 The Shakespeare Service.*

William Boyton Kirk was the son of a well-known Dublin sculptor and had come to the attention of Kerr and Binns when he obtained a prize at the Society of Arts in London. Kerr and Binns looked to Kirk to help re-vitalise the company and, as Kirk was an enthusiastic admirer of Shakespeare, plans were made to illustrate *A Midsummer Night's Dream* by means of an elaborate dessert service. This service was a resounding success at the Dublin Exhibition of 1853.

The modelling skills of Kirk were also evident in many other projects. One example of this was an 1856 advertisement which proclaimed the 'Illustrious Warrior' being a parian brooch featuring the profile of Wellington, modelled by Kirk, and fitted in a Moroccan leather case.

26 An engraving of the works during the Kerr and Binns period (viewed from the Bath Rd.).

The engraving in fig. 26 probably dates back to 1852 and was done for the purpose of illustrating an early guide to the works. The engraving also features in an article on the Royal Porcelain Works in *The Official Illustrated Guide to the Great Western Railway* of 1860. This article includes some interesting facts about the company: 400 persons employed (50 of which are females in the burnishing department); wages between 30 shillings and £5 per week; and nine large kilns. It also states that the *Great Eastern* have entrusted their ware orders to the Company who have of late years been engaged in the manufacture of a class of ware called 'Vitrified Stone China' for hotel and shipping as well as family purposes; its great peculiarity being enormous strength.

Thomas Bott was an eminent artist-craftsman who was partly responsible for the company's improving fortunes in the 1850s and 1860s. His arrival at Worcester was apparently fortuitious for he had gone job hunting in Bristol only to find that his prospective employers had gone out of business. On his return journey home there was a stop-over in Worcester where he was informed of the local porcelain works and the following day he duly went to the works armed with examples of his drawings. He was immediately engaged as a figure painter and his skills were developed at the Worcester School of Art. Before long he was given the task of decorating large porcelain pieces in enamels based on the famous Limoges style.He was also entrusted with vital decorating work on the Shakespeare Service .

Bott was known as a man of gentle disposition and was a popular well regarded employee. Bott did not enjoy the best of health and he died in December 1870 just a few months after suffering a stroke.He was only 41 years old. He lived in the London Road area of the City and is believed to be buried in Astwood cemetery.

27 Thomas Bott.

Other important employees of the Kerr and Binns period included William Taylor (painted floral subjects including Australian heathers), Josiah Davis (the renowned gilder who later did important work on the Chicago Vase), and modellers such as E.J.Jones and C. Toft. Other well regarded painters and decorators included David Bates (floral subjects), Stephen Lawton (enamel and gilt decorator), Robert Perling (landscapes), Josiah Rushton (figure subjects), and Luke Wells (dogs and other subjects and who also did painting work on the Shakespeare Service).

Kerr and Binns took particular advantage of the Worcester School of Art which had opened in Pierpoint Street under the patronage of the Earl of Dudley in October 1851. Many of their apprentices were sent there for training and these included Josiah Rushton, John Hopewell, James Sherriff junior, James Hadley, Samuel Ranford, George Gibbs, and the Callowhill brothers.

Thus the seeds had been sown for the future and the resulting crop was to be artistry of the highest quality.

28 Josiah Davis, Thomas Bott, & William Taylor.

ROYAL PORCELAIN WORKS,

Worcester, March, 1862.

IMPORTANT SALE.
Worcester Porcelain.

MESSRS. KERR & CO. beg to inform the Nobility and Gentry, and Families Furnishing, that a Change of Partnership being about to take place, they have determined on disposing of the whole of their Manufactured Stock by Private Sale, at Reduced Prices, or Discount, at the Works, consisting of

BREAKFAST,
DINNER,
DESSERT,
TEA, and
TOILET SERVICES,

In Fine Porcelain, and Stone China.

The above are made into Services, for 12, 18, or 24 Persons, and all marked in plain Figures, at Reduced Prices.—The Ornamental Stock will be sold subject to Discount, according to amount Purchased.

The Stock is chiefly of the newest and most elegant Patterns, and almost every variety of Prices, in value amounting to from £20,000 to £30,000.

SALES FROM 9 A.M. TO 6 P.M. EACH DAY,
FOR A LIMITED PERIOD.

SAMPLES FORWARDED, CARRIAGE FREE, IF REQUIRED.

☞ ALL SERVICES PURCHASED AT THE ABOVE SALES CAN BE MATCHED HEREAFTER AT THE MANUFACTORY.

N.B.—VISITORS ADMITTED TO INSPECT THE WORKS AS USUAL.

LONDON OFFICE: 91, CANNON STREET, CITY.

DUBLIN: 114 & 115, CAPEL STREET.

29 Advertisement from The Art-Journal Advertiser *in early 1862.*

The achievements of the Kerr and Binns period should never be underestimated: vital new buildings had been constructed (see fig. 34), a workforce of only 70-80 had been increased to about 400, and artists and craftsmen of the highest quality had been assembled to drive the company to new heights of perfection. Financially the company was pushed to the limit by all this progress and the above sale was held in 1862 to inject much needed capital into the company. However, further measures than this were needed to sustain the growth and prosperity of the company.

The Worcester Royal Porcelain Company
1862-1897

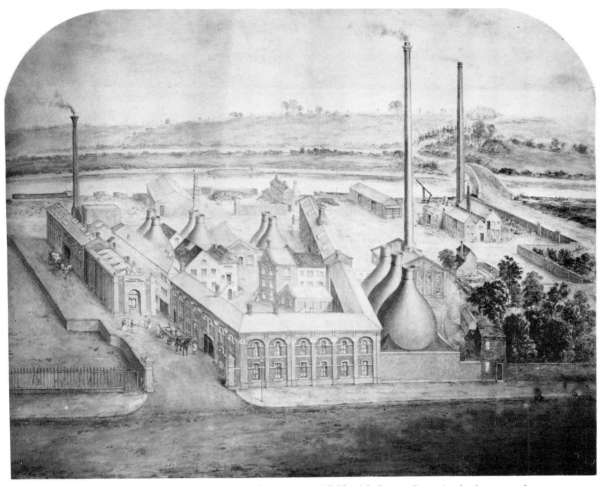

30 The Worcester Royal Porcelain Company in 1868 with Severn Street in the foreground.

The future of the Diglis factory was effectively secured by the formation of the joint stock company in June 1862. The hard work of the Kerr and Binns period was rewarded by the attraction of important new subscribers to the concern. These were Edward Phillips (a Staffordshire potter of repute), William Litherland (a Liverpool china merchant), and local dignataries: Martin Abell, Peter Hardy, Richard Padmore, Alexander Sherriff, William Adcock, and Thomas Southall. R.W. Binns was given a directorship and was to control artistic production.

Although times were difficult expansionism was still seen as the only way forward and by 1865 plans were laid to increase the size of the operation still further. The Diglis site was to be abandoned and new premises were to be built on part of the former Worcester Public Pleasure Grounds sited in the Arboretum area (see fig. 31). One interesting aspect of this scheme is that the six local Royal Worcester directors above were all directors or shareholders in The Worcester Public Pleasure Grounds Company Limited! As that company had gone into liquidation in early 1865 this was obviously seen as a way of killing two birds with one stone. Mr. Adcock duly bought the Pleasure Grounds for £8,500 and the Worcester Porcelain Company then purchased them from Adcock for the same figure. Raising the necessary finance to build the new premises evidently became an insurmountable problem and in the end Adcock was forced to buy back the Pleasure Grounds for the same figure again! One can only surmise that Adcock was a man of considerable wealth which was probably fortunate for a company in danger of over extending itself financially. Nevertheless expansion was not hindered by these events as extra land surrounding the Diglis site was soon bought up and more new buildings were erected. In fact parts of the new proposed design were actually incorporated in the extensions as can be seen in the Severn Street frontage as shown above.

31 Proposed new porcelain works in the Arboretum. Only half of the grounds would have been required for the works and the lower part of the plan illustrates the grounds as they were then. The lodge building can still be seen in Sansome Walk today.

The building partly obscuring the showroom and Severn Street frontage in fig. 32 is the school of St. Peter's which was built in 1843. It is interesting to note that it has been removed from the view of the works shown in fig. 30. Its proximity to the Company's prestigious showrooms must have been an embarrasment in some ways and when plans were made to extend the school in 1891 the company ensured that the extension was away from their property by giving the school land to the north on which to build their new wing. This led to the demolition of several cottages and the aptly named Royal Porcelain Works Inn.

32 A view of the porcelain works taken from the Cathedral tower around 1880.

St. Peter's School closed down in the late 1950s and in 1965 the 1843 and 1891 old school buildings were bought by the Dyson Perrins Museum Trust and they now form the basis of the present day museum. The main hall of the school and one of its largest classrooms form the main showrooms while the headmaster's room is now the office of Curator Harry Frost.

St. Peter's Church, situated nearby was demolished in 1976 and the grounds are now part of the factory site.

33 Royal Porcelain Works Inn.

PLAN OF WORKS 1876

A - Finished Warehouse
B - Lodge
C - Archway
D - Packing House
E - Show Room
F - Passage
G - China Sliphouse
H - Common Sliphouse
I - Aluminium House and Clay Store
J - Lumber Store
K - Painters Shop
L - Stores
M - Stove
N - Potters Workshop
O - Boiler House
P - Engine House
Q - Gearing Room
R - Wash Tub
S - Grinding Shop
T - Mould Chamber
U - Insulator Oven
V - Biscuit Oven
W - Coal Yard
X - Block containing Painting & Printing Departments
Y - Future Site of Museum

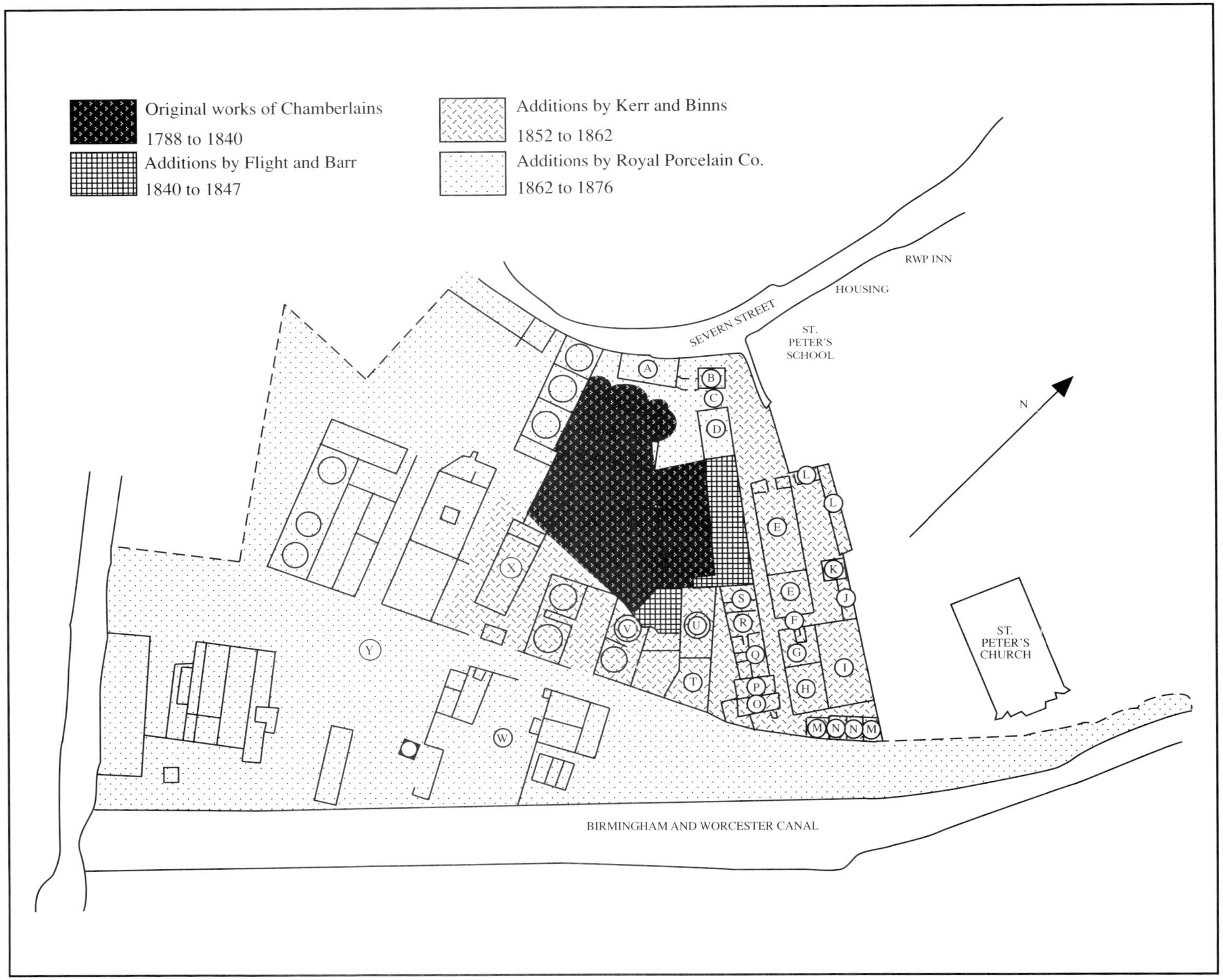

Original works of Chamberlains 1788 to 1840

Additions by Flight and Barr 1840 to 1847

Additions by Kerr and Binns 1852 to 1862

Additions by Royal Porcelain Co. 1862 to 1876

ST. PETER'S CHURCH

RWP INN

HOUSING

ST. PETER'S SCHOOL

SEVERN STREET

BIRMINGHAM AND WORCESTER CANAL

N

34 *Plan of the works adapted from an old map photographed by George Evans, Tallow Hill, Worcester. Unfortunately not all of the buildings are identified.*

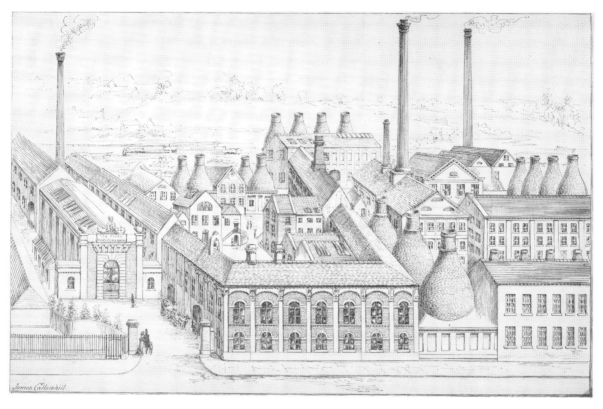

35 Drawing of the works in around 1881 (by James Callowhill).

36 James Callowhill.

James Callowhill was born in Worcester in 1838 and was one of the first successful pupils of the Worcester School of Art. He was a typical example of the fine artists produced by the school (also known as the Worcester Government School of Design). Much of his work was used at exhibitions and he specialised in figure subjects, heads and the art of chased gilding where agate was used to scratch patterns on gold. His younger brother Thomas Scott Callowhill (born 1841) was also a gifted artist and decorator who specialised in Limoges enamel painting for some time as well as doing similar work to his brother. Both brothers specialised in raised gold storks incorporating chased gilding. James drew several exterior and interior views of the works while at Worcester and these were used to illustrate early *Littlebury's Guides to Worcester*. It is possible that they were also used in some of the early guide books to the works but the style of these does seem to differ very slightly from that of Callowhill.

The Callowhill brothers emigrated to the U.S.A. in the 1880s and their talents were lost to Worcester forever.

37 A view of the works in around 1890 with the Bath Road in the foreground.

38 A view of the works in around 1895 taken from the Cathedral tower.

39 An early view of the potting department. This photograph and the three following were all taken by the London Stereoscopic & Photographic Company Ltd., who were based at 106 & 108 Regent Street, and also 54 Cheapside. There must have been at least 17 photographs taken in this series but only the four depicted survive today.

40 (right)
An early view of the gilding department. Note the gilding wheels in the foreground.

41 (below)
An early view of the burnishing department.

*42 Another early
view of the
burnishing
department.*

The influence of R.W. Binns continued throughout the remainder of the nineteenth century. Here was a man of rare talent who combined managerial ability with artistic and historical knowledge. An excerpt from the *Art Journal* of July 1873 reveals the esteem with which Binns was regarded: '...every one who has watched the career of the present indefatigable manager, Mr. R.W. Binns, cannot but feel that this notable factory is not likely to lose in fame while in his hands. A master of his art from every point of view, that is to say chemically, technically, and artistically, and a reliable authority in all that relates to the literature of the potter's art, Mr. Binns pursues his vocation with an earnestness and a judiciousness which insure success. Since the beginning of the decade which witnessed his introduction to the proprietary of the firm, Mr. Binns has given us a constant succession of agreeable surprises; recognising fully the fact that exactly in proportion to its capability of receiving decoration, porcelain judiciously treated, even in the smaller pieces, becomes highly decorative; and that, without losing sight of its

43 R.W. Binns FSA (1819-1900).

44 Worcester Japanese porcelain at the Vienna Exhibition (from The Illustrated London News, *Nov. 1, 1873). The accompanying article accredits R.W. Binns with the design and production of these articles; ably seconded by his chief modeller, artist, and chemist, Messrs. Hadley, Callowhill, and Bejot (to whom medals were awarded). A Diploma of Honour was awarded to the Company.*

45 The suite of plate in electro-art silver presented to R.W. Binns in recognition of 25 years service.

application to the wants of every-day life, it can be made to add a charm to the domestic arrangements of the table, and enrich either the costliest or humblest furniture.'

Binns was also instrumental in the opening of a chemical laboratory at the works in 1873. This was in recognition of the fact that as wares became finer the firing process became very important in producing perfection. Binns also looked at experiments with gas used as fuel and visited the Royal Porcelain Manufactory laboratories in Charlottenburg in this connection.

Binns never rested on his laurels and he was always examining the competition to ensure that the Company was not missing out on new developments. Consequently he often bought examples of his rivals ware at exhibitions for study and analysis by his own staff.

Mr. Binns returned from the Centennial Exhibition held at Philadelphia in 1876 armed with examples of high quality Japanese porcelain. These were duly shown alongside Worcester wares at the Worcester Public Hall and it was during that occasion that Mr. Binns was to be given a surprize presentation of a suite of plate in electro-art silver consisting of a pair of salvers and a ewer. This was accompanied by a fulsome address lavishly illustrated by the Callowhill brothers. The Chairman of the Board of Directors - Mr. A.C. Sherriff - made the presentation while the address was read out by the senior foreman of the men's painting department - James Sherriff. In reply, Mr. Binns made his maxim of the previous 25 years - 'aim high'- an even shorter one of just two letters - 'XL'. One wonders if Mr. Binns was generally a man of few words!

At the Paris exhibition of 1878 Worcester was not only awarded a Gold Medal for its efforts, but Binns was granted the coveted Cross of the Legion of Honour. This was then followed by a Gold Medal award at the Melbourne Exhibition of 1881. Personal tragedy followed for Binns in 1882 when his talented young son, Albert, died at the age of 20 years. He had fallen from a damson tree but death was apparently from peritonitis caused by swallowing a damson stone.

A further extension to the works came in 1884 when land opposite the main entrance in Severn Street was purchased and a Works Institute was constructed. This was provided for the well-being and education of the employees and various classes and lectures were arranged covering topics such as reading, music, elocution, religion, botany and art. The Works Institute also incorporated separate mess-rooms for male and female employees. The provision of such a facility in Victorian times illustrates the concern the directors had for their employees and while Binns himself was a man of benevolence, evidence suggests that Edward Probert Evans, the Company Secretary from 1867, did much to influence Binns in this direction. Indeed Evans was instrumental in the formation of the Royal Porcelain Works Sick Club in 1874 and the Employees Benefit Fund in 1879. He also arranged occasional trips to the seaside. Evans was rewarded for his efforts by being promoted to Manager in 1887 and to celebrate his twenty years service with the Company a presentation evening was held in his honour at the Public Hall.

The vast influence of Binns was severely diminished in the 1890s after he suffered serious illness in 1891. His retirement inevitably came in 1897 and his respectful employees presented him with a beautiful illuminated address in book form lavishly illustrated by painters of the ilk of John Stinton, Charles Baldwyn, George Johnson and Edward Salter. Binns, however, remained a director of the Company and would often make the short journey from Diglis House to the works which he probably felt was his true home. Before he died in 1900 he managed to complete his final work for Worcester in the form of his scarce book *Worcester China, a record of the years 1851 to 1897*. William Moore Binns (his youngest son) succeeded him as Art Director in 1897.

46 R.W. Binns features prominently in the centre of this photograph probably taken about 1890. Second person from his left is one of the gilders who features in fig. 128 while fourth person from his left is Samuel Ranford. On the back row can be seen William Hawkins (eighth from the right) and George Glover (sixth from the right - tall man with beard). George Glover (1853-1904), a salesman and clerk , was a relative of E.P. Evans. Samuel Ranford (1839-1909) started at the works in 1852 and is regarded as one of the finest gilders of the nineteenth century. He was foreman of the gilders for some years. He died of heart failure following diabetes in January 1909.

47 A fine study of R.W. Binns in his study at Diglis House.

Diglis House was the home of the Binns family for several years but it soon changed hands after the death of R.W. Binns in 1900. By 1908 it was a small brewery and licensed premises and I rather wonder if the great man would have been impressed by the change of use!

A Guide Through The Works

48 The cover of the 1853 guide.

The early prints and photographs that exist today of the workrooms at the Diglis factory were produced originally for the very good reason of illustrating the guides to the works. The earliest guide that has been found in the archives dates back to 1853 but unfortunately only the cover and an interior view of the showroom remain of this important document. However several guides from the 1870s remain fully intact and it is from these that the prints in this chapter are largely obtained. These prints provide an admirable insight into the various processes involved in manu-facturing porcelain in the mid to late nineteenth century and it is interesting to compare them with the photographs used in the guides dating from the turn of the twentieth century.

Some earlier prints are also shown and these accompanied an article called *A Day at the Royal Porcelain-Works, Worcester* which appeared in *The Penny Magazine* of February 1843.

49 The interior of the showroom as depicted in the 1853 guide.

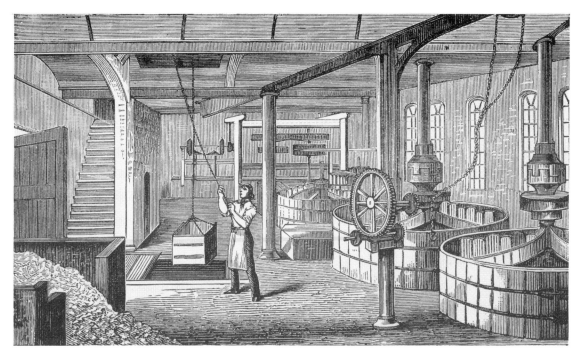

50/51 The Mill showing the first floor.

The Mill department consisted of a boiler-house, engine-house, and the mill, a three-storied building. The large pans shown were for grinding flint, felspar, Cornish stone, etc. There were also pans for grinding the glazes, and a series of smaller ones for colours. The time necessary for grinding the different materials varied from 12 hours to 6 days!

52/53 The Slip Room or Slip House.

Underneath the floor of this building were the large arks which acted as reservoirs for the substances from the mill and clay house. Here were the mixing pots into which the ground materials were thrown by pumps. After being thoroughly sieved the material or slip was then pumped into a clay press whereupon water was expressed by hydraulic pressure until the mass assumed the consistency of paste. This was then taken to the clay cellar where it was beaten and kneaded to make it tough.

54 Potter's wheel with Thrower, Ball-maker and Wheel-turner at work (Penny Magazine).

Once the proper consistency and homogeneity had been imparted to the clay it was ready for the workman. In the old guide books the usual methods of manufacture were stated to be 'throwing', 'pressing', and 'casting',the two former with the clay in a state of paste, the latter when in a state of slip.

The 1875 guide book described the 'throwing' process as follows: 'Plain circular articles, such as cups and bowls, are made on the potter's wheel by the thrower. This apparatus is of great antiquity. In the tombs at Thebes (dating about 3,800 years ago) have been discovered drawings which exhibit the potter's art in a variety of forms: the kneader of clay, the baller, and the thrower.

The man who works at the potter's wheel is called the thrower. He receives from his assistant a ball of clay, which he throws upon the head of the wheel or horizontal lathe before him, and presses it with both hands; the rotary movement causes the clay to rise in the form of a stalk or cone which he then depresses and again allows to rise. When the clay is thus made ready, he inserts his thumb into the mass, moulding and fashioning the outsides with the other hand. In this way cups and bowls are formed. The thrower having formed the cup or 'lining' as it is called, afterwards presses it into a mould. In a short time this mould will have absorbed sufficient moisture from the clay to allow it to become detached; it is then taken out and is ready for the turner.'

The turner fixed the ware upon his lathe, and treated it much the same as he would a piece of wood or metal. He finished the edge and foot, and, if necessary, the outside surface. The form of the cup completed, it was then passed to the handler.

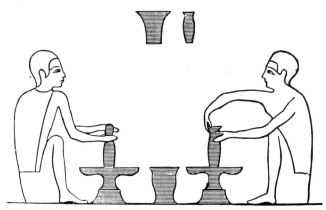

55 The Egyptian Thrower. The action of the thrower was the same but motive power was provided by the left hand applied directly to the wheel.

56/57 The Thrower.

Handles were pressed in moulds, whether for tea-cups or vases, and underwent the process of trimming and fitting, which was speedily done by the workman who next proceeded to fix it on the cup with a little liquid clay called slip. The clay acted as a cement, and, being of the same material, united the two parts when burnt in the oven. All objects with handles went through a similar process.

58 Fixing Handles (Penny Magazine).

59 Fixing Handles.

60 Plate Making.

The manufacture of plates and dishes is called flat pressing. For plates the clay was weighed into balls, which were extended out into flat discs like pancakes. The mould that gives the form to the face of the plate or saucer was fixed in a horizontal lathe called a jigger. It was then covered with a disc of clay, which was then pressed firmly to the mould while it revolved very quickly. The workman then took a tool called a profile which was fitted to the edge of the mould, and when this was pressed in the centre caused the foot to rise in a perfect circle. The mould with the plate upon it was then placed in the stove to dry. When the heat caused the plate to contract from the mould, it was taken off and finished in a semi-dry state; it was then ready to be burned.

61 The Pressing Room.

62 Hollow Ware Pressing.

The manufacture of soup tureens, covered dishes, ewers and basins, and the like is called hollow ware pressing. These objects were all made in moulds. The workman first prepared a slab of clay, and having carefully placed it in the mould he bossed it with a wet sponge into every marking and line. The mould after a little time absorbed sufficient moisture to allow the clay to contract, and the piece was then easily removed.

63 Figure Making Department.

Casting, one of the most interesting processes of potting, is shown in the figure-making department. When a figure had been finished by the modeller it was cut into pieces to be moulded. The mould maker was careful to ensure that each part was extracted from the mould in perfect condition and with as little seam as possible. A figure when cut up and moulded could easily be represented by 20 to 30 moulds, each containing a separate part.

Liquid slip clay with the consistency of thick cream is then poured into the orifice of the mould. When sufficient slip had adhered to the mould the remainder was poured back into the casting jug. The slip having remained in the mould for some minutes was then sufficiently solid for the workman to handle. He then arranged all the pieces on a slab of plaster in front of him and trimmed any superfluous clay from each piece. He then applied liquid slip to the parts making sure each joint was perfect and gradually built up the whole figure. Superfluous slip was removed with a camel's hair pencil. The object was then propped with various clay strips with the same shrinkage properties and was then ready for the oven.

64 Figure Making.

65 Kiln Placing House.

66 Placing.

42

67 Putting manufactured articles into saggars
(Penny Magazine).

68 Placing the saggars in the Biscuit Kiln
(Penny Magazine).

The manufactured articles were then ready for firing and were taken to the placing house of the biscuit oven. Here they were placed in strong fire-clay saggars, shaped to suit the different wares, and these protected the wares during the firing. Flat objects were bedded in exact forms prepared for them in ground calcined flint, a substance which did not melt or stick to the china. Hollow pieces (cups and bowls etc.) were placed together in oval saggars and ranged on china rings to keep them straight. The saggars were then very carefully placed one over the other in the oven. This was absolutely necessary as when the oven was heated to a white heat (calculated as equal to about 25,000 degrees Fahrenheit) the least irregularity of bearing might have caused a pile to fall to one side and affected the firing of the whole oven and caused great damage. A china oven was built of fire bricks and was generally about 14 feet in diameter inside and had about eight fireplaces. Firing occupied about 48 hours and cooling about 40 hours. Small test cups drawn through holes in different parts of the oven showed the fireman (by contraction and the various degrees of translucency) the progress of the firing.

The porcelain was then in a state called biscuit, and having had the flint rubbed off the surface, and been carefully examined, was then sent to the dipping room.

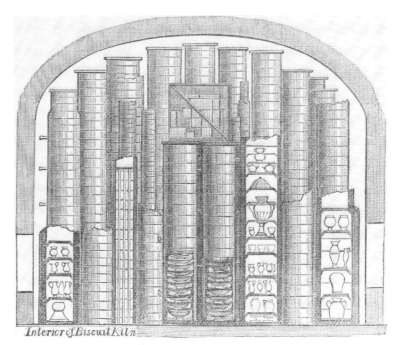

69 Interior of Biscuit Kiln.

70 *The Dipping Room.*

The dipping room contained large tubs of various glazes (which had been ground on the mill for about ten days), to suit different wares. Here the ware was dipped in the glaze by a practised hand, who was careful that it was evenly distributed over the surface. The ware was then taken to the stove to dry, and was afterwards carefully examined in the trimming room, so that any superfluous glaze could be removed before it was taken to the glost oven placing-house.

The glost oven was of similar construction to the biscuit oven; it took 16 hours to fire, and was allowed 36 hours to cool; after which the ware was taken out, and sent to the white ware rooms, where it was sorted and stored until required for decoration by the printers, painters or gilders.

71 *Glazing (or Dipping).*

Printing on porcelain had a long tradition at Worcester and a whole team of artists were employed to engrave on copper plates the patterns supplied by the designers. Underglaze colours were fired in the glaze kilns, and overglaze colours in the special kilns or muffles used for painted and gilt work.

44

72/73 Printing and Transferring department.

74/75 The Painting Room.

The painting department was probably the most interesting for the visitor as they were able to watch the now famous but then humble painters engaged on subjects such as landscapes, birds, and flowers. The gilders would then enrich their work with the adornment of gold. After the first 'wash in' of the colours (which were prepared from metallic oxides) had been burned, and the painter had worked upon it for the second fire, the forms and finish both in style and colour began to appear. Painters were trained from the tender age of 13 years under special instructors who imparted to them not just the ability to draw but also an understanding of the manipulation of colours and the action of the fire upon them.

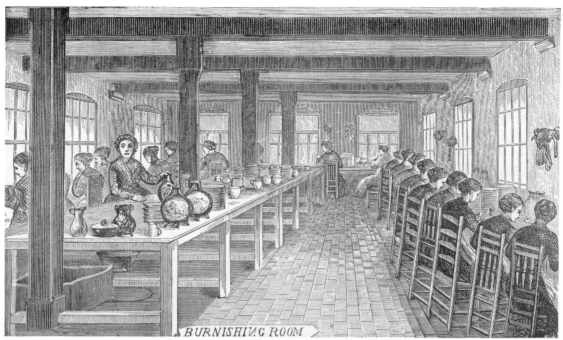

76 The Burnishing Room.

77 Burnishers at work.

When the ware was drawn from the enamel kiln the gold was of a dull colour but once it had been carefully cleaned and a burnisher of bloodstone or agate had been quickly rubbed over it, it assumed the beautiful bright appearance of burnished gold.

The processes of manufacture today do not necessarily differ greatly from those described. However, semi-automation of many of these processes has taken place. Decorating processes have also changed relatively little over the years.

Diversification of manufacturing has occurred at various times. Notably during the 1840s Chamberlain's manufactured china door furniture and buttons. Neither of these ventures proved profitable but at least a venture into tile manufacture proved somewhat useful.

Grainger's also diversified their manufacturing at times and unusual products included false teeth, sauce bottles, gas meter dials, telegraph insulators and even a 'Patent Drawing Room Flower Pot'.

78 *Making the tiles.* (Penny Magazine).

79 *Tessellated tiles. (Penny Magazine).*

The *Penny Magazine* of February 1843 also discussed the manufacture of tessellated tiles at the Worcester works. R.W. Binns attributed this to the awareness of Walter Chamberlain:

'Mr. Chamberlain was a clever potter and a most ingenious man; he therefore undertook to do battle with the Staffordshire opposition, by producing the commoner class of goods. Varieties of bodies and glazes were invented in order to rival the earthenware of Staffordshire, and special bodies were produced for toilet ware and other branches of the trade; but, notwithstanding all the exertions which were thus most laudably made, the trade continued to decline.

One of Mr. Chamberlain's schemes was to reproduce the encaustic tiles of the middle ages. This most interesting branch of manufacture had in olden times been carried on in the county, and the enterprising proprietor consequently hoped that prestige as well as profit would result if the speculation could be brought to a successful issue.

The undertaking was successful, and was carried on for many years by the wet clay process as well as by the dry.....'

After the 1840 merger the tile business was moved from the Diglis factory to the old Warmstry factory under the close attention of the Barrs and F. St. John. Subsequently the business was sold to Messrs. Maw , who moved the manufacturing process to their Benthall works, near Ironbridge in about 1853.

Grainger's, Hadley and Locke

The third porcelain factory to appear in Worcester was the firm of Thomas Grainger in the early 1800s. Thomas was a grandson of Robert Chamberlain (the founder of Chamberlain's) and served his apprenticeship with the family firm. The company was based in Saint Martin's Gate in Lowesmoor but suffered a very early blow when the premises burned down in the space of two hours on the 25th April 1809. However all was not completely lost and new premises were built nearby soon afterwards. Thomas was assisted in his business by a number of different partners from time to time. His original partners were Stephen Wilkins (a wealthy vinegar merchant) and John Wood (a former Chamberlain's painter). Later partners were John Lee (his father-in-law), Benjamin Crane (his stepfather), James Pardoe and James Lee (son of John Lee).

80 George Grainger (1812 or 13 - 1888).

Thomas died in 1839 and the business was then run by his widow, Mary Ann, and son George. He soon became the dominant figure in the business and introduced a new type of porcelain

81 Grainger workforce c. 1894. Back row, second from left: Bill Jordan (an ornamental presser who made large vegetable dishes). Third from left: Edward Locke? Front row, first from left: Walter Blissett (a kiln worker who later worked at the Diglis factory and died around 1930). Second from left: Alfred Barry. Also in the photograph is a Mr. Hollinshead.

82 *George Grainger stands proudly outside his premises at 19 Foregate Street, Worcester. Later the shop of W.H. Smith and now a pizza parlour.*

manufacture in 1848 called 'semi-porcelain' or 'chemical porcelain'. The company had a successful display at the Great Exhibition in 1851 where this new type of porcelain was shown. Further success followed at the London International Exhibition of 1862. This was partly due to the skilled reticulation techniques of Alfred Barry who was responsible for the fine show of pierced parian wares. While Barry cannot be considered in quite the same class of workmanship as George Owen he was, nevertheless, a fine exponent of the art of reticulation. Barry worked for Grainger's for many years and transferred to the Royal Porcelain Works in 1902 staying there until his retirement in 1907.

83 Alfred Barry at work.

Although Grainger's was probably never the largest porcelain factory in Worcester at any time during its history it is interesting to note that the 1861 Worcester Census records that there were between 30-40 men & boys employed and 10-12 women & girls employed at Grainger's. When Binns recalled his arrival at the Diglis factory in 1852 he suggests that staffing was in the region of only 70-80 employees although , of course, he soon remedied that situation. But for Kerr and Binns it is not inconceivable that Grainger's would have become the dominant porcelain business in Worcester!

George Grainger was a successful businessman of his time and he was also prominent in local life serving both as a town councillor and magistrate. George died in 1888 after suffering ill health for a long time and he was duly given a glowing tribute in the local press. His son Frank sold the firm to the WRPC in March 1889. Grainger's retained its own identity until 1902 when the staff were removed to the main factory at Diglis.

The Grainger premises were eventually auctioned off in March 1903 by George Yeates & Sons of Worcester. The original sale particulars still survive and make interesting reading:

By direction of the Worcester Royal Porcelain Company, Limited.

ALL THAT
IMPORTANT FREEHOLD MANUFACTORY AND WORKS
FORMERLY KNOWN AS

GRAINGER'S ROYAL CHINA WORKS,

Situate in ST. MARTINS GATE, WORCESTER, within five minutes' walk of the centre of the City, and Shrub Hill Railway Station, and three minutes of the Worcester and Birmingham Canal.

GENERAL REMARKS

Lots 1 and 2 will first be offered in one Lot, and if not then sold will be offered in two Lots as described below.

The splendid position of these important properties, combined with the extensive areas and frontages to three streets near the centre of the City and Railway Station, cannot fail to recommend them to the best attention of Manufactures and Investors.

There is plenty of labour to be obtained close at hand for any new business which may be started on these Premises.

Purchasers will have the great advantage of

POSSESSION OF EACH LOT ON COMPLETION.

No part of either of the Lots is to be used for the manufacture or Sale of porcelain, China, or Pottery of any kind, and a provision to this effect is to be inserted in the Conveyance of each Lot

An interesting plan accompanied the particulars of sale and the various buildings and plots were described, briefly, as follows:

LOT 1. COMPRISED - 1. DRIVEWAY ENTRANCE, having a pair of folding doors. 2. A QUITE MODERN TWO-STOREY BUILDING, containing - Timekeeper's Office, two large and well-lighted Warerooms, and Office over entrance. 3.PACKING HOUSE and STRAW LOFT over. 4. PACKING SHED and lock-up OIL STORE. 5.POLISHING SHOP and GAS ENGINE HOUSE. 6. TWO PRINTING ROOMS. 7. Portion only of a THREE-STOREY BUILDING, comprising two Decorating rooms and two lavatories. 8. A THREE-STOREY BUILDING, comprising - Ware placing room, Glaze-dipping room, Potting room, two stoves, and Mould room. 9. TWO OVENS. 10. SMALL DAMP ROOM.

Nearly the whole of the buildings above are brick built with slated or tiled roofs, and some of them were erected only seven or eight years ago. The total area of Lot 1. was in the region of 1379 square yards.There was also a large yard.

LOT 2. COMPRISED 11. THE REMAINING PORTION of the THREE-STOREY BUILD-ING, numbered 7 in LOT 1, containing-Burnishing Room,two w.c.'s, two Pattern rooms, and Decorating Room. 12. A TWO-STOREY BUILDING, comprising Ware room, and capital modern Show Room. 13. & 14. THREE ENAMEL KILNS and PLACING HOUSE. 15. SMALL DECORATING ROOM. 16. MOULD MAKING ROOM. 17. FOUR w.c.'s and URINALS. 18.OPEN SHED. 19. SAGGAR HOUSE and STOVE. 20. BLOCK MOULD ROOM. 21. BISCUIT OVEN PLACING ROOM. 22. PLACING ROOM with POTTING ROOM over. 23. HOVEL and KILN. 24. BONE KILN, BONE STORE, POTTING ROOMS, and STORE ROOMS. 25. & 26. TWO LEAN-TO STORE SHEDS. 27. WAREROOMS, MODELLING ROOMS, OFFICE, and COLOUR STORE. 28. SLIP HOUSE with DRYING KILN. 29. A MODERN KILN AND SHED not included in the sale and to be removed by the vendors. There was also a large yard.This Lot was said to be suitable either for a Manufactory or for conversion into a really excellent building site for artisans' dwelling houses(Such houses being close to the railway station and various works and factories would readily let !). Total area of this Lot was in the region of 2551 square yards.

84 The frontage of the Grainger Factory today.

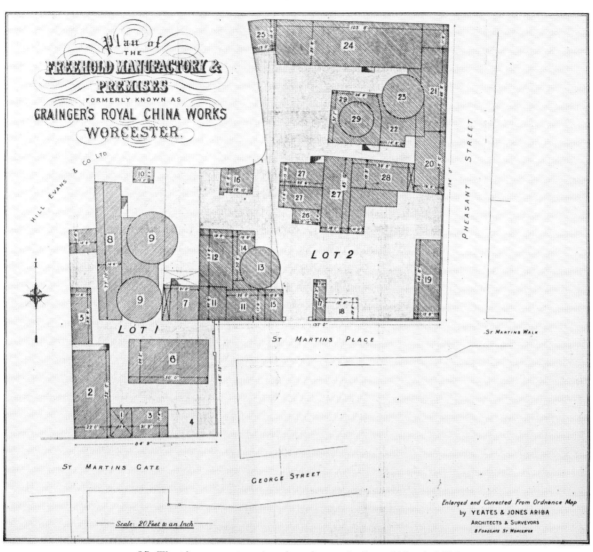

85 The plan accompanying the sales particulars of March 1903.

86 The last surviving part of a bottle kiln in Worcester. This is the the left hand side of the more southerly of the two ovens marked 9 (fig. 85).

87 The young James Hadley (1837- 1903).   *88 James Hadley. Photo by T. Bennett & Son.*

By comparison with the Grainger factory the life of the Hadley factory was very short-lived. Nevertheless the nine years of its operation from 1896 to 1905 saw the production of some fine art pottery and 'faience'. The founder of the company was James Hadley who some regard as one of the greatest ceramic modellers of the nineteenth century. Hadley's family were actually hairdressers and James was initially intended to be a hairdresser! As a boy James was apprenticed to the Royal Worcester Porcelain Company and soon became one of it's most eminent modellers. He decided to leave the company in 1875 and set up his own local studio in the High Street, concentrating on modelling and design. However most of his work was bought up by his old employers and it was not until 1896 that he decided to start his own porcelain factory. James concentrated on producing wares he called 'faience' and this product was continually developed giving rise to the term 'Hadley ware' which was clearly different to the wares produced by his old employers.

Financial backing was provided by Frank Littledale and the company became Limited in 1900. James did not participate in the public life of the City but he was musically inclined and was known to be friendly with the Elgars who also had premises in the High Street.

89 Hadley advertisement in the Pottery Gazette *of 1st July 1898.*

90 *The Diglis works of James Hadley and Son. Roland Blake is standing by the milk churn and was a foreman at the works. He later did pierced work in the style of George Owen at the WRPC. Two large kilns can be seen to the rear of the main building.*

91 *Howard Hadley (1862-1929). Photo by A.J. Neale.*

James had married Louisa Wilks in 1860 and they had five sons. All were baptised at the Countess of Huntingdon's Chapel. Henry was born in 1861 but only lived to 1865. Howard was born in 1862 and educated at the Worcester Royal Grammar School. He married Florence Simes , a member of the well- known local drapery store family, in 1889. Howard worked as a modeller and designer for Hadleys and subsequently for the WRPC but is probably better remembered for his fine contribution to local activities. He was a violin pupil of Sir Edward Elgar and a leading member of the Worcester Amateur Operatic Society. He was also founder of the Worcester Boys Brigade and an active member of the Angel Street Congregational Church. He died at the age of 66 years after a long period of illness.

92 A Hadley factory outing to the Malvern Hills around 1900. James Hadley can be seen in the left foreground with a walking stick. Immediately behind him with flat hat and tie is Frank Hadley. Louis Hadley is standing in the right foreground while Howard can be seen in the boater and bow-tie in the middle right of the group.

93 Frank Hadley (1873-1958).

Louis Hadley was born in 1865 and was a successful pupil at the Worcester School of Art where he he was particularly adept at flower studies. A number of his drawings (as well as some of his fathers) are now in the possession of the Dyson Perrins Museum. He is thought to have run the London office of Hadleys.

Harry Hadley was born in 1866 but did not have a direct interest in the porcelain industry.

Frank Hadley was the youngest son and he became the decorating manager for Hadleys and later worked for the WRPC. He never married and died in 1958.

James Hadley suffered from ill health in the early 1900s and was taken seriously ill in December 1903. Death from peritonitis soon followed. The heart had be torn from the new company and it was not long before the WRPC acquired it in 1905. Hadley style wares were very popular with the public and the Company continued to produce such wares for many years to come. Indeed painters were often trained to paint in the Hadley style and well known amongst these were Kitty Blake, Millie Hunt, Albert Shuck, Horace Price and Walter Sedgley.

94 The Locke factory today - now in various industrial uses.

Another short-lived porcelain manufactory in Worcester was that of Edward Locke's which was situated in Newtown Road, near the bridge where the railway line crosses the road. Edward (1829-1909) was a Grainger's employee for many years but decided to form his own company in 1895. He took with him other members of his family including Kate Locke (his daughter) who was a pate-sur-pate painter of considerable ability (Edward himself was an artist and master potter). Also enticed away from the now Royal Worcester owned Grainger factory were two of the Stinton family, Arthur and Walter.

Locke's factory was purpose built and the two main buildings, both of two storeys, had a total area of 13,000 square feet. This was a serious manufacturing operation backed by local businessmen, John Stallard junior and E.L.Adlington. Locke's concentrated on smaller pieces specifically aimed at the lower end of the market but they also made more ornate objects. Of particular interest was their range of heraldic or 'crested' china which is considered to be of a superior quality to that produced by other manufacturers.

Locke's incurred the wrath of the WRPC in 1902 because of their use of the word Worcester on their wares which it was felt was confusing the general public into thinking that Locke's was Royal Worcester. A famous High Court case ensued which the WRPC won. An appeal was lodged but settlement between the two parties was achieved privately beforehand.

95 Locke Worcester China in a Malvern shop window.

57

ROYAL WORCESTER AND OTHER WARE.

ROYAL WORCESTER VASES.   Rose Bowls, Plaques, Pot Pourri Jars—Vase and Cover.

Small Royal Worcester CUPS	... ...	1/6, 1/11, 2/6, 3/11
Royal Worcester SALVE BOXES	... ...	1/6, 2/11

Royal Worcester VASES, 3½-inches high	6/11, 8/11
Royal Worcester JUG, Gold Handle, 5-inches high ...	6/11
Royal Worcester LOVING CUP, 3 Handles, 5 by 5-inches ...	16/9
Royal Worcester Miniature VASES, 3¾ and 4½-inches, in various shapes	6/11
Royal Worcester VASES, 4½-inches, Dragon Handle..	12/9
Royal Worcester EWER VASES, 5-inches, Solid Gold Handle	6/11
Royal Worcester EWER VASES, 5½-inches, Solid Gold Handle	10/6
Royal Worcester VASES, 7-inches, Grecian shape ...	15/6
Royal Worcester VASES, 9-inches, Prettily Embossed, Spill shape	21/-
Royal Worcester VASES, 10½-inches, Chelsea bottle shape ...	33/-
Royal Worcester EWER VASE, 10½-inches, Head Handle and Solid Gold Handle	37/6
Royal Worcester VASES, 9-inches, Egyptian bottle shape ...	21/-
Royal Worcester URN VASE, with Cover, 12-inches, Two Handles	52/6
Royal Worcester VASES, 9-inches, Ewer shape, Very Choice, Very Artistically Embossed	45/-
Royal Worcester VASE, with Cover 1½-inches	39/6

• POT POURRI JAR, 13-inches, with Dome Cover, 92/6

Royal Dresden TEA SETS, £4 10s. 0d.

Royal Dresden PLAQUES, Hand-Painted, 63/-

Cameo Ware, Pot Pourri Jars, Vases, Urns, Plaques, Etc.,

BY LOCKE & CO., SHRUB HILL WORKS, WORCESTER.

POT POURRI JAR, 6-inches high, Parian Body, Hand-Painted and Raised Gold Leafage 14/6

PLAQUES, 10-inches, Fawn and Pink Parian Body and Hand-Pierced 10/6

VASES, 4½-inches, square shape, Raised White Cameo and Gold	1/11
VASES, 5-inches, Prussian Blue, Parian Body, with Raised White Cameo	3/11
POT POURRI JARS, 5-inches, Cameo Ware, with Hand-Pierced Dome Cover	4/11
Cameo-Covered URN, 6½-inches, and Burnished Gold Handle ...	4/11
EWER VASE, 5½-inches, Raised White Cameo	3/11
VASE, 10½-inches, Celadon Green, Parian Body, with Raised Cameo and Traced Gold	15/-
VASES, 12-inches, Hand-Pierced Top, Silver-Grey Parian Body, and Traced Gold	9/11
VASES, 13-inches, Dark Green, Parian Body, Raised White Cameo, and Traced Burnished Gold	25/-
EWER VASES, 4½-inches, Pencilled Ivory and Traced Gold ...	3/11
EWER VASES, 9-inches, Hand-Pierced Top, Biscuit Shaded, Hand-Painted Birds and Raised Gold Relief...	6/11
VASES, bottle shape, 10½-inches, Pencilled Ivory, Fawn Shaded, and Raised Gold Passion Flower	21/-
VASES, fan shape, 5-inches, Hand-Pierced Decoration and Russet Shaded	7/11
VASES, 12-inches, with Cover, Hand-Painted Wild Rose and Bronze Burnished Gold	35/-
VASES, 14-inches high, Parian Body, and Raised Gold Passion Flower	42/-

1, 3, 5 and 7a, CHURCH ST.,
2 and 4, WHITECHAPEL,   **BUNNEY'S Ltd.,**   **LIVERPOOL,** **And at LLANDUDNO.**

96 A Full-page advertisement in a catalogue issued by the Liverpool based department store of Bunney's Limited in the early years of this century. This fully illustrates the reasons behind the Royal Worcester Porcelain High Court action. It would be quite possible from this advertisement to imagine that it was Locke & Co. who actually made Royal Worcester wares! Locke's continued production for some years after the case but eventually closed down in 1915 when the factory was bought by the local printing firm of Ebenezer Baylis and Sons.

Factory Buildings 1900 - 1951

97 *The impressive facade of the Royal Porcelain Works in the early twentieth century.*

98 *An old part of the works. The building on the right was to become the Chamberlain Tea Rooms.*

99 *A close-up view of the future Chamberlain Tea Rooms.*

100 The Severn Street view of the works around 1900.

101 The canalside at the works around 1906.

102 The Chamberlain Tea Rooms as etched by Harry Davis and reproduced as a postcard.

Some of the oldest buildings on the Diglis site were converted into the Chamberlain Tea Rooms in 1931 and these were to prove highly popular with visitors. It is interesting to note that when they were opened on the 16th of April 1931 it was said that as they were part of the original Chamberlain buildings it was inconceivable that they would ever be pulled down. After World War II, however, the company decided to demolish most of the original Chamberlain buildings and this included the Chamberlain Tea Rooms!

A measure of the importance of the Tea Rooms in the 1930s can be gauged from the fact that they were one of the subjects chosen for a set of six postcards published by Raphael Tuck & Sons Ltd. The other five subjects were The Central Show-room, Throwing, The Ovens, Dipping, and Gilding.

The original Tea Rooms sign depicted Robert Chamberlain but it is actually the profile of Humphrey Chamberlain. The sign was the work of Harry Davis and has recently been rediscovered by Harry Frost while he was clearing out a stockroom! The sign can be seen in figs. 102 and 105.

103 Raphael Tuck's postcard of the Chamberlain Tea Rooms.

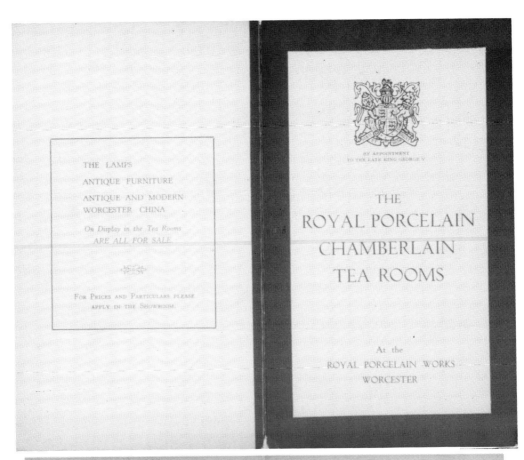

104 *Chamberlain Tea Rooms menu of the 1930s.*

105 Finished wares being taken to the showrooms. Photograph by Fox Photos, 8 Tudor Street, London, May 1932.

108 (above) An interior view of the works with the original Museum buildings built in 1879 on the right. The Museum and the office of R.W. Binns were on the top floor.

106/107 (above) Two views of black and white buildings that used to adjoin the St. Peter's Street entrance to the works.

The proud kilns of Worcester, the embodiment of porcelain manufacture to the layman, met an inglorious and unheralded end in the post World War II period. More efficient and cleaner gas-fired tunnel kilns brought about their demise but also produced ware of a finer quality. Unfortunately none of the familar bottle kilns have been preserved for prosperity and now our only reminder of a somewhat grimy past is the forgotten remains of a kiln hidden among the industrial buildings at Saint Martin's Gate (see fig. 86).

109 Death of a kiln.

Exhibitions, Royalty and Museums

110 The audience at the closing ceremony of the Worcestershire Exhibition on October 18th 1882. Showcases of Royal Worcester porcelain can be seen alongside the wall. Grainger's also displayed their wares at this exhibition. Photo by Norman May of Malvern - photographer to the exhibition.

R.W. Binns was a great believer in the value of exhibitions and used them as an important way of enhancing the Company's reputation and prestige which, in turn, would lead to a greater demand for their productions. Binns commented: 'The great International Exhibition of 1851 sounded an awakening throughout the United Kingdom. Manufacturers began to perceive their deficiencies and all seemed anxious to profit by the object lesson so splendidly placed before their eyes'. The public were also awakened by the Great Exhibition and purchasers were no longer content to buy only what the dealer had to sell but made enquiries for new productions. The Dublin exhibition of 1853 was the first chosen by Kerr and Binns to provide opportunity to enhance the Company's reputation. The Shakespeare Service proved a great success at Dublin and further success also followed at the London International Exhibition in 1862. Rival manufacturers were now well aware of a revived Worcester Royal Porcelain Company.

111 John Dynon & Son of 43, Lonsdale St. were the agents at the Melbourne Exhibition.

112 The Prince and Princess of Wales leaving Witley Court for Worcester in 1884.

The Company's reputation was also enhanced by visits from royalty and these included Queen Adelaide in 1845, the Queen of the French in 1858, the Prince and Princess Christian in 1870 and, most notably, the Prince and Princess of Wales in 1884.

113 The Prince and Princess of Wales at the Guildhall, Worcester.

114 A lavishly decorated porcelain works awaits the arrival of the Prince and Princess of Wales.

115 The Chicago Vase.

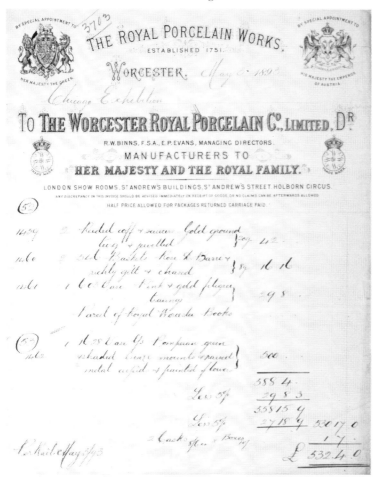

116 The Chicago Vase Invoice.

Considerable success was gained at several exhibitions, notably at Vienna in 1873 when the highest possible award (The Diploma of Honour) was obtained, and at Paris in 1878 when a Gold Medal was awarded.

Spurred on by these successes a large display was duly planned for the colossal exhibition to be held at Chicago in 1893. Binns commented: 'This experiment was looked forward to with much interest, for never before had so grand an undertaking been dreamed of in what many regarded as the wild west. Prophets of evil were not wanting, and doubts were freely expressed as to the feasibility of the scheme. The result is a matter of history, and it can only be said that, whatever may have been the financial outcome, Chicago outshone all her rivals in the grandeur of the conception and the beauty of the execution of her *World's Fair*.'

The Company was lucky in being given an important frontage position within the English section. Amongst the mainly fine and costly wares on display was the largest vase ever made in Worcester porcelain - the famous Chicago vase which now sits proudly in the Dyson Perrins Museum. To make such a large vase was a daunting task and the whole process took one year to complete. The vase was modelled by James Hadley while moulding was the reponsibility of John Finney. Edward Raby was chosen to paint the depiction of the four seasons in Art Nouveau style, and gilding was by Josiah Davis. Mr. W. Moore Binns superintended the decoration of the Chicago vase and all the other main Royal Worcester exhibits.

117 Edward Evans (son of E.P. Evans), F. Farmer (standing), and Charles Amphlett pictured by the Niagara Falls during the Chicago Exhibition in April 1893. Close examination of the photograph suggests that this was probably a studio study with the background superimposed later!

118 Worcester Royal Porcelain Exhibition stand in New Zealand in 1906-7.
Photo by Wheeler & Dutch, Christchurch, New Zealand.

119 Some of the exhibits at the Franco-British Exhibition, White City, London in 1908.

120 The Company's stand at the Franco-British Exhibition.Photo by Arthur E. Smith.

121 A close-up view of some of the exhibits. This photo and fig. 119 by J. Benjamin Stone.

A special excursion to the Franco-British Exhibition was arranged for employees on the 4th of July 1908 at a cost of 6 shillings. The train departed from Shrub Hill station at 5.45 a.m. and did not return from Paddington until after midnight. This was because the Exhibition remained open until 11.00 p.m. and the company wanted their employees to fully benefit from their visit!

122 A view of the showroom around 1876. Photo by George Evans, Tallow Hill, Worcester.

123 A selection of wares especially made for the Chicago Exhibition on display in the showroom.

124 The original museum in the 1890s. In the background is a drawing of lilies by Edward Raby.

The establishment of a museum at the Worcester Royal Porcelain Works was due entirely to the efforts of R.W. Binns. Binns was a man of great antiquarian interests and shortly after his arrival at Worcester he began to collect specimens of old Worcester porcelain. Binns wanted to assemble a complete illustration of the history of the manufactory and was as interested in the ordinary productions as much as the more exceptional works. One piece of good fortune in the formation of the collection was that a Worcester broker had bought much of the old stock of the Warmstry factory when it had closed and Binns was able to purchase this at a later date being very aware of its historical importance. Some items were so primitive that it was considered probable that they formed part of the original Doctor Wall

125 The original museum around 1902.

trials! For some years this collection was stored in the private office of Binns but eventually it was realized that a more spacious home was needed. Furthermore Binns had now amassed a large collection of wares from other factories that he had bought to inspire his workers and they also needed a permanent home. Accordingly the Directors of the Company opened the Museum in 1879. This was a purpose-built building which also incorporated a new office for Binns.

126 (right) Showcase of Worcester porcelain at the South Australian National Art Gallery & Museum around 1900. Photo by Ernest Gall.

At Work and Play

A number of the important workers in the early history of Worcester's porcelain have already been discussed and this chapter therefore concentrates on the workers of the late nineteenth century and the first half of the twentieth century. Unfortunately the museum archives do not contain photographs of all the famous characters of that period and so, inevitably, there are some omissions. Nevertheless most of the well known 'names' appear in the following selection of photographs.

Josiah Davis (see fig. 28) is thought to have completed about 60 years service at the works. This fine designer and draughtsman certainly lived through a time of great change at Worcester encompassing the changes wrought by Kerr and Binns, the great increase in the size of the operation between the 1850s and 1870s, and then finally the slide towards depression in the early twentieth century. Josiah is perhaps best remembered for his gilding on the Bott enamels and his scroll work on the Chicago vase.

Josiah's immense talents were fortunately inherited by his offspring. One son, George, specialised in raised work while another, Alfred, was a china presser. Alfred, however, was the father of the renowned Harry Davis (1885-1970)!

John Osborne is to be remembered for his sheer length of service to the Company. He worked between 1871-1945 (he was at Grainger's for a time) and was in charge of the pattern room for some years (see figs. 128, 141 & 142).

127 Josiah Davis (1839-1913).

128 Royal Worcester gilders around 1888. Photograph by Percy Parsons, St. Nicholas St., Worcester. On the back row second from the left is Mr. Green who started at the works in 1877 at the age of 15 years. On the back row second from the right is John Osborne (1858-1947).

129 George Owen in his workroom (1845-1917).

George Owen is recognised as the finest reticulator in the history of Worcester porcelain. Reticulation is the painstaking and difficult art of piercing porcelain in order to produce works with an appearance of lace-work. This form of ceramic decoration is extremely intricate and time-consuming and George must have been a man of great patience and solitude. George had to work at all times with soft clay, and needed to operate skilfully and quickly on each section before the clay dried. Due to the size of many of his works this would have meant keeping many of them in a green state (a term for moist workable clay) for many weeks or months. This coupled with the knowledge that a momentary lapse in concentration could ruin a piece of work reveals the cool composure and immense ability of the man. He was fortunate, however, in being ambidextrous.

George was Worcester born and bred and lived at 12, Wood Terrace in the Arboretum for many years where among his neighbours was a certain James Stinton! George's work gave variation to the product range Royal Worcester was able to offer and his work featured prominently in the Company's worldwide exhibitions. Particular emphasis was placed on his work at the Franco-British Exhibition of 1908.

Edward Raby was the son of Samuel Raby who was a flower modeller in the 1860s and 1870s. Edward was a floral artist of great ability. He thought that roses were the queen of flowers and loved painting them. A contemporary admirer commented: 'looking (the roses) as if they had been freshly picked from a tree with the dew still heavy upon their living petals'. Edward worked at Worcester between 1875-83 and 1884-96 when he left for the Royal Doulton China Works. He was an uncle of Harry Davis and had close links with the Angel Street Congregational Church.

In the photograph below the foreman of the painters was the well regarded William Hawkins (1858-1930). He started at Worcester in 1874 and soon progressed to foreman status in 1881. He was a specialist in portrait and figure subjects, and still life studies. He was also active in the social life of his workers, sometimes holding parties at his house in Sebright Avenue. He was also a prominent member of the cycling club.

130 Edward Raby (1863-1940).

Frank Roberts (1857-1920) started at the works in 1872 and was a fine fruit painter. Charles Baldwyn (1859-1943) started in 1874 but left in 1909 to become a freelance water-colourist. He must be regarded as one of the finest painters of birds (particularly swans) on porcelain. His water colour paintings were often exhibited by the Royal Academy. When he married in 1897 his best man was William Hawkins. George Johnson (1859-1931) was a good friend of 'Charley' Baldwyn and they often used to go on walking and sketching trips into the countryside to places like Trotshill, Oddingley and Hawford. George also specialised in painting bird subjects.

131 A fine study of Royal Worcester painters around 1899. Back row, left to right: Frank Roberts, Charles Baldwyn, George Johnson, Richard Sebright, Charles Greatbach (flower painter - left for Locke's in 1904), William Hawkins, William Hale, William Ricketts. Middle row (seated): Thomas Sadler (flower painter), Robert Rea (painted landscapes, flowers & butterflies), Edwin Salter (landscape & fish painter tragically killed in 1902). Front row (seated): Harry Davis, B. Richardson (both apprentices at this time).

132 An austere view of the painters room around 1910. Left to right: Thomas Lockyer, William Hawkins, Richard Sebright, Raymond Rushton, Ernest Phillips.

133 Harry Davis (left) and Harry Stinton (1883-1968) sketching by the banks of the Severn.

Harry Stinton was a son of John Stinton junior and started his employment at the Grainger factory in 1896 before transferring to the main factory in 1902. Harry Davis was a good friend of his and they used to go on fishing trips together. Stinton is now highly regarded not only as a porcelain painter but also as a water-colour painter of great ability. The main subject of his work on porcelain were Highland cattle (the same main subject as his father). He retired from the factory in 1963.

Harry Davis was apprenticed to Edwin Salter who not only passed on his talents to a willing and able pupil but also his love of fishing! In 1900 Harry won a prize for a roach he had caught on the river Teme at Shelsley and also a South Kensington National Book prize for a water-colour study of that same fish. Harry soon became an outstanding painter and was made

foreman when Hawkins retired in 1928. Subjects he painted include sheep, fish, polar bears, Highland cattle, pigs, landscapes, snowscenes, and scenes of London. His reputation among lovers of Worcester porcelain is probably unsurpassed.

Richard Sebright was a quiet unassuming man who must be regarded as one of the finest painters of fruit on porcelain to have worked at Royal Worcester. He worked at Worcester for 64 years retiring through ill-health in the late 1940s. Like so many of the Royal Worcester painters he also painted water-colours and he exhibited at the Royal Academy. These were principally flower studies of elaborate detail and are highly considered today. Earning money was of secondary interest to him and as a result he would spend many hours more than his contemporaries on similar pieces of work. A devout bachelor, he was always held in the highest regard by his colleagues.

134 Richard Sebright (1868-1951).

135 Richard Sebright at work towards the end of his illustrious career.

136 W.A. Pointon (1860-1941), a renowned figure maker and modeller, joined Worcester in the mid 1870s as an apprentice and is shown here still working at the age of 72 years in 1932.

137 Furniture painted by Walter Austin (1891-1971). He was a well known Worcester painter who served his apprenticeship under William Hawkins. He painted mainly flower subjects (also fruit and fish) but there was little work for him in the depression and he left the company in 1930. He managed to find some part-time work with the local furniture firm of Rackstraws which involved painting panels of flowers and fruits on varnished sideboards, dressing tables, wardrobes and the like. Apparently some of these were made for use on large ocean liners.

Eight of the Stinton family are known to have been involved in painting on porcelain. Both Henry Stinton and his son, John Stinton senior, worked at Grainger's. John Stinton senior retired about 1895 but three of his five sons also became ceramic painters. The oldest of these was John Stinton junior (1854-1956) who started his career at Grainger's before moving over to the main factory in 1902. He was an extremely fine landscape painter and specialised in cattle and Highland cattle scenes. He retired in 1938 and can be seen in figs. 140 & 142. Walter Stinton was the fourth youngest of the five sons and is thought to have been about two years older than his youngest brother, James. Walter was also employed at Grainger's but left in 1895 to join the new enterprise of Edward Locke. He subsequently left the porcelain industry completely and died in 1950. James (1870-1961) was also a Grainger's employee (unfortunately he rarely signed his work there) and like his elder brother, John, he moved to the main factory when the Grainger's factory was closed. He specialised in the painting of gamebirds (notably pheasants and grouse).

The three other painting Stintons were the offspring of John Stinton junior: Arthur (1878-1970) who worked at Grainger's and Locke's; Kate who painted at the Royal Porcelain Works; and Harry who has already been discussed on page 78.

138 Walter Stinton & granddaughter.

The black and white house to the left of James Stinton in the photograph was once the proposed site of a new showroom for the Company. These plans were never implemented and, sadly, this quaint house was demolished in recent years (see also figs. 106 and 107).

139 James Stinton strolls along Sidbury during his retirement.

140 Royal Worcester painters pose for the camera on the occasion of William Hawkins retirement in 1928. Back row, left to right: T. Lockyer, A. Shuck, H. Price, R. Austin. W. Bee, J. Stanley, H. Ayrton. Second row: C. Creese, H.Everett, W. Powell, E. Sharples, W. Long, J. Freeman, A. Halford, E. Barker, R. Rushton, G. Moseley, W. Bagnall, E. Townsend, H. Davis, W. H. Austin, H. Stinton, James Stinton, E. Spilsbury, J. Hendry, W. Sedgley. Front row: Kitty Blake, R. Sebright, E. Phillips, W. Ricketts, W. Hawkins, G. Johnson, John Stinton,W. Hale, Millie Hunt.

Thomas Lockyer started with the company before World War I and stayed with them until he tragically committed suicide in 1935. He was a specialist fruit painter in the style of Frank Roberts. Albert Shuck (1880-1961) was Hadley trained and painted pheasants, fruit, orchids and other flowers. Horace Price (1898-1965) painted Hadley and Worcester style flowers. Reginald Austin (1890-1955) specialised in birds, flowers and fruit subjects who, like his brother Walter, left the Company in 1930. William Bee (fruit), Jack Stanley (flowers,figure subjects and still life), and William Bagnall (fruit and still life) left in the 1930s through lack of work.Harry Ayrton (1905-76) worked for the company between 1920-70 and painted fruit, fish, horses etc. Charlie Creese painted rural scenes, Cathedrals and also did work on the early Lindner horses. Miss Hilda Everett was a flower painter who left in the early 1930s. William Powell worked between1900-50 and was a specialist in British birds. John Freeman was a long serving talented fruit painter. Ernest Barker (1890-1958) was trained under Harry Davis and specialised in flowers and sheep. Raymond Rushton (1886-1956) was a fine landscape and architectural painter. George Moseley worked between the World Wars as a fruit and bird painter. Ted Townsend (1904-78) was a popular painter (fruit, sheep, birds, cattle & fish) who became foreman of the men painters in 1954. Miss Ethel Spilsbury was trained in the Hadley style and painted flowers. James Hendry was a landscape painter of Scottish origin. Walter Sedgley worked for the company between 1889-1929 and specialised in flowers and general subjects. Kitty Blake was a popular character who worked from about 1905-53. She specialised in blackberry subjects and Hadley style flowers. Ernest Phillips and William Ricketts both specialised in flowers.William Hale started with the Company in 1874 and died in 1930. He was a fine all round decorator. Millie Hunt specialised in Hadley style flowers.

141 A group of long serving employees around 1929.

Back row, left to right: Fred Lipscomb (gilder), Albert Glover, Richard Sebright, William Blake , Albert Charles Darling (traveller) , -?-, W. Rushton, Leonard Burgess (introduced and developed process of acid printing), William Hale (painter), J. Baylis (printer). Front row, left to right: George Beare (printer), Miss Brown ?, Mrs. Hardman, John Osborne, Mrs. Charlotte Davis (mother of Harry and a transferer and paintress), Anne Pointon (sister of William), William Pointon (modeller).

142 Another group of long serving employees around 1937.

Back row, left to right: R. Russell (saggar maker), W. Blake (foreman potter), William Davis (design department), J. Haywood (retail show room and traveller), W. Jordan (potter - see fig. 81), W. Scrivens (foreman of printing department),William Evans (gilder), W. Lewis (engraver), John Stinton junior (painter). Front row: W. Rushton (potter), A. Davis (potter), Mrs. Hardman (cleaner?), John Osborne (see figs. 128 & 141),Richard Sebright (see figs.131,132,134,135,140 &141), Albert Charles Darling.

143 The Royal Porcelain Works Cycling Club pictured outside the show room around 1890.

The Royal Porcelain Works Cycling Club was probably formed in the early 1880s (an entry in the diary of Henry Baldwyn, the father of Charles , mentions one meeting in April 1885 when members met at the house of Mr. Evans at Barbourne Bank). It had as many as 75 members between 1892-1894. For reasons unknown the club folded soon after this but was temporarily revived in 1920. A few of the cyclists in the above photograph can be identified with some certainty. The man with the large black beard in the centre of the photograph is Mr. E.P. Evans, while the third person to his right is William Hawkins. The small man with a beard immediately to the left of Hawkins is William Moore Binns (manager decorator). Third person to the left of Mr. Evans is Eli Haywood (side-profile with beard). He ran the showroom and was the father of John Haywood (see fig. 145) Immediately to Haywood's left is the light bearded man who also appears in figs. 92 & 93. Directly under the middle of the window frame is Ernest Davis - the engraver and uncle of Harry Davis. Immediately to his right is Samuel Ranford (seated on bike with beard).

The Royal Porcelain Works Cycling Club.

President: Mr. W. A. HAWKINS.

Fixtures for 1920.

Captain: Mr. G. F. Harrison.
Sub-Captain: „ W. Powell.
Secretary: Miss M. L. Spilsbury.
Treasurer: „ L. Bradley.

Committee:
Mr. T. Morton.   Mr. H. Price.
„ A. Shuck.   Mrs. K. Shuck.
„ G. Evans.   Miss N. Raginbeau.

Rear-Guard Signals:
1. Leader to slacken speed: *Whistle once.*
2. To Halt: - *Whistle continuously.*

POTTER PRINTING CO. ALL HALLOWS, WORCESTER.

FIXTURES FOR 1920.					Remarks
Date	Day.	Route.	Start sharp at	Starting Place	Lighting up.
June 29	Sat.	Old Storridge	2.30 p.m.	Wor. Bridge	
„ 24	Thur.	Stoulton	7 p.m.	Bath Road	
„ 26	Sat.	Stourport	2 p.m.	R'd h'se Droitw'h rd	
July 1	Thur.	Droitwich	7 p.m.	R'd h'se Droitw'h rd	
„ 3	Sat.	Upton	2.30 p.m.	Wor. Bridge	
„ 8	Thur.	Old Hills	7 p.m.	Wor. Bridge	
„ 10	Sat.	Evesham	12.45 p.m.	Bath Road	Wet
„ 15	Thur.	Tibberton and Hindlip	7 p.m.	Shrub Hill Stn.	Enjoyable Ride
„ 17	Sat.	Tewkesbury	2 p.m.	Bath Road	5 turned up
„ 22	Thur.	Pershore	7 p.m.	Bath Road	Road Rice.
„ 24	Sat.	Malvern	2.30 p.m.	Wor. Bridge	home
„ 29	Thur.	Crown E. via Broadh'th	7 p.m.	Wor. Bridge	good Road
Aug. 12	Thur.	Ombersley and Holt	6.30 p.m.	R'd h'se Droitw'h rd	home
„ 14	Sat.	Ankerdine	2 p.m.	Wor. Bridge	
„ 19	Thur.	Trotshill	6.30 p.m.	Shrub Hill Stn.	
„ 26	Thur.	Fernhill Heath	6.30 p.m.	R'd h'se Droitw'h rd	
„ 28	Sat.	Inkberrow	2.30 p.m.	Bath Road	
Sept. 2	Thur.	Kempsey	6.30 p.m.	Bath Road	
„ 4	Sat.	Old Storridge	2.15 p.m.	Wor. Bridge	
„ 9	Thur.	Norton	6.30 p.m.	Bath Road	
„ 11	Sat.	Malvern	2.15 p.m.	Wor. Bridge	

144 The Royal Porcelain Works Cycling Club Fixture List for 1920.

145 *The Royal Porcelain Works Cycling Club around 1920 (possibly a Malvern trip in September 1920). Left to right: Miss Cam, -?-, Mr. Harrison (club captain), Miss Nellie Raginbeau(nurse), Miss Thatcher, Miss Fildes, George Evans, Miss Millie Hunt, May Bloodsworth, Mr. J. Haywood, William Hawkins (club president - seated in front), Miss L. Bradley, Harry Davis, -?-, Miss M.L. Spilsbury, Miss Marjorie Wall, Mr. Cam (fitter), William Powell. William Hawkins was involved in both eras of the club and was club captain in the early days. Photo by A.J. Neale.*

146 *Before dinner!*

An interesting feature of the porcelain workers is that their artistic talents did not just lie within the realms of their work. Many of them painted as a form of relaxation (or as a means of earning much needed extra money) and several famous characters exhibited at the Royal Academy. Others were accomplished amateur musicians and social occasions would often include musical interludes of one form or another. Several of the Grainger workforce were known to be musically inclined and they even formed their own band and travelled around local hostelries and villages. Apparently they would often finish their musical outings opposite George Grainger's shop in Foregate Street and regale him with their rendering of *The Fine Old English Gentleman*. George was known to play the flute and I wonder if he ever joined in this event!

Musical talent also existed among the Hadley family. James Hadley was a friend of the Elgar family, and was also an enthusiastic flute player, while Howard Hadley's musical talents have already been discussed. In his diary Henry Baldwyn often mentions appointments to tune pianos at the various Hadley households. In the 1880s musical lessons were held at the Works Institute and the above photograph (on the reverse is written 'before dinner') probably dates from that period. We do not know who the musicians are but close examination of fig. 46 suggests that some of them are also in that photograph albeit slightly older! It was evidently usual to have musical entertainment at most social events and this will be seen in the menus shown on pages 88 & 89.

148 1908 advertisement from Littlebury's
Worcester and District Directory.

Photography was also a hobby for some workers but in the case of Arthur Neale it was also a supplement to his income. Arthur was designated Works Photographer and was allowed to do his own private work. Harry Davis recollected that his earnings per week were all of £1 out of which he was stopped two shillings superannuation. Arthur was responsible for the photographs featured in figs. 91,127 and 145.

147 Promotional visit of the Daily Mirror Pages in around 1926.

149 W.R.P. hockey team around 1930.
Centre back row is Libby Griffiths. This was organized by Miss Ayres who features in figs. 155 & 160.
She was affectionately known as 'Nan' and started at the works in 1925 at the age of seventeen years.
Nan also ran a 'keep fit' class. During World War II she ran a Red Cross department at the works,
manned the first aid post, and arranged lodgings for war workers at the factory. In the evenings she
helped to tend the wounded soldiers at Ronkswood Hospital. She used to cycle to Broadheath, where
she ran a Brownie pack. Nan retired in 1968 after 43 years of service.

150 Worcester carnival float entered by the Company in around 1930. Pekin was a well known pattern of that period.

151 Carnival participants pictured outside the Chamberlain Tea Rooms. Mrs Doris Sear (née Mountford) is seated fourth from the left on the front row. Photographs featured in figs.149,150, 151 and155 are by courtesy of Mrs Sear.

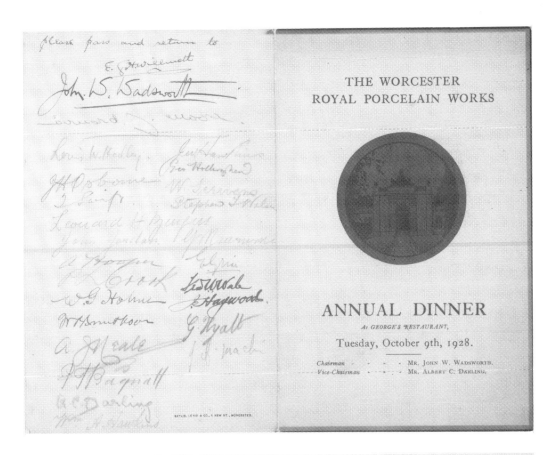

152 First Annual Dinner Menu.

Despite the depression of the late 1920s a First Annual Dinner was arranged in 1928. Perhaps this was arranged to cheer up the workers of a company in great difficulties. It was reported as a successful affair and that the length of service of those present totalled nearly 800 years! Major B.J. Moore regaled the assembly with a report on his recent visit to the U.S.A. where he hoped to obtain more business for the company. The signatures of those present can be seen on the menu above.

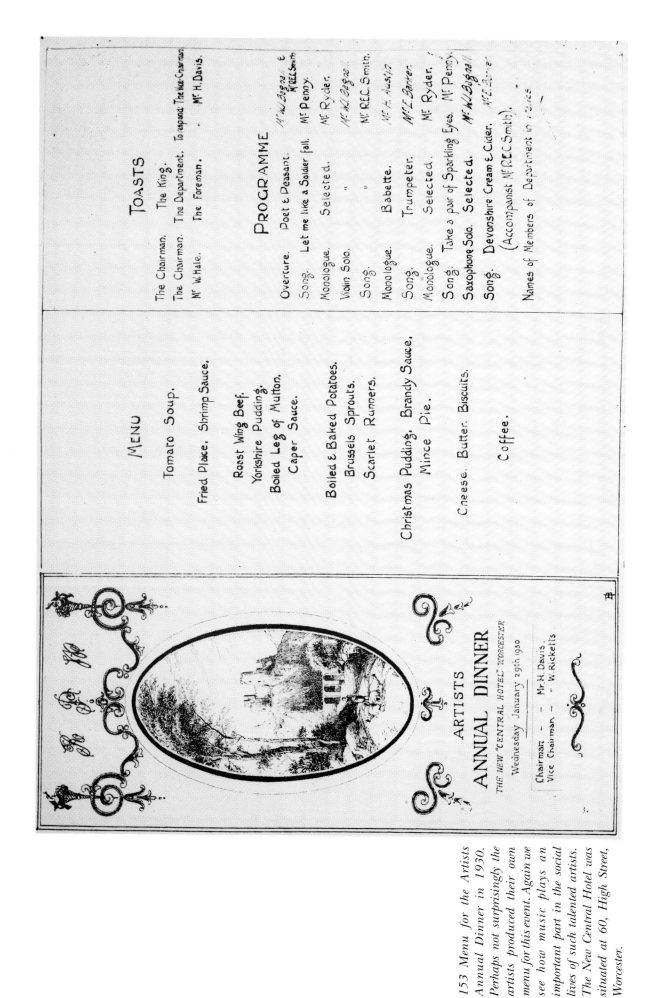

153 Menu for the Artists Annual Dinner in 1930. Perhaps not surprisingly the artists produced their own menu for this event. Again we see how music plays an important part in the social lives of such talented artists. The New Central Hotel was situated at 60, High Street, Worcester.

154 The Porcelain Works ambulance team in the late 1940s.
Back row, left to right: Paul Rado, Reg Griffiths, Reg Reeves, -?- , -?- , -?- . Front row: Bruce Teague, Archie Garner,
Bill Smithson, Mr. Wearmouth, -?- , Jim Beechey. Photo by W.W. Dowty.

155 An award winning team of nurses at the Royal Porcelain Works in July 1948.
Left to right: Mrs. M. Hemming, Mrs. D. Telford, Miss A. Ayres, Miss M. Brown, Miss M. Avery.

Dyson Perrins

156 Dyson Perrins - Mayor of Worcester in 1897. Photo by T. Bennett & Sons.

Charles William Dyson Perrins (1864-1958) was the only son of five children born to the wealthy James Dyson Perrins of *Worcestershire Sauce* fame. He was educated at Charterhouse and Queen's College, Oxford and then spent four years in the Highland Light Infantry before entering the family business. When his father died in 1887 Dyson Perrins inherited a vast fortune which he was to administer with admirable responsibility and philanthropy.

He became a director of the WRPC in 1891 his interest aroused by his hobby of collecting old Worcester wares. Thus started his lifelong association with the Company which was not only to secure it's survival but also to permanently establish a superb museum collection for future generations to enjoy.

Dyson Perrins first came to the rescue in 1898 when he loaned the Company the princely sum of £20,000 on a first mortgage of the factory. He was elected to Chairman in 1901 and continued to give considerable financial assistance to the Company which was struggling through the difficult times of World War I and the following years of depression. In the 1920s he often made up the wages of the workforce and in 1927 he even purchased the museum collection off the Company for £15,000 in a bid to bolster it's finances. This figure was in excess of its real value and the collection was still to remain in the museum! Despite these benevolent acts, however, the Company was soon in the hands of the Receivers and it was not until Dyson Perrins purchased the Company outright that its survival was ensured. The new Company was formed in 1934 with Dyson Perrins as Chairman. In 1946 he created a Museum Trust to administer and unite his own mainly early collection of Worcester wares and that of the Museum's which was mainly Victorian and early twentieth century in character.

157/158 Dyson Perrins outside the Guildhall on the occasion of being made a Freeman of the City in 1937. The store of Freeman Hardy Willis was formerly used as a retail outlet by Samuel Bradley (one of the original 15 partners of the Worcester Tonquin Manufacture) for the sale of Worcester wares and also by Chamberlain's for a period of time from 1789. In the top photograph can be seen Dyson Perrins' second wife, Frieda. Other famous Freemen of the City of Worcester include Lord Nelson, Sir Winston Churchill and Lord Nuffield.

159 Dyson Perrins on holiday.

160 Dyson Perrins, Miss Ayres, and Mrs. Perrins outside the showroom in 1941.

Perhaps the pinnacle of Dyson Perrins life came on June 8th 1951 when the future Queen opened the Dyson Perrins Museum. He was then Company Chairman and had the honour of escorting the Princess around the museum which she had opened with a special gold key. After the departure of the Princess a grand Bi-centenary Dinner was held at the Guildhall. There were 496 persons present, including the vast majority of the employees and directors of rival firms. Mr. J.F. Gimson (Managing Director) gave a special toast to Mr. Dyson Perrins: 'For 60 years he has been a director. Without him, there would have been no company, no prosperity, and no Bi-centenary. His love of Worcester china, his financial support and unfailing enthusiasm had brought the company through many crises to a leading position in the pottery industry today.'

Dyson Perrins retired from the Board in 1954 but remained Honorary President until his death in 1958.

161 Dyson Perrins guides Princess Elizabeth around the new museum.

162 Princess Elizabeth hears from Mr. Gimson some of the secrets of the casting process.

163 A Worcester craftsman at work on an equestrian statuette.

94

Bibliography

Much of the text in this book has been derived from the Dyson Perrins Museum's own archives. However, many excellent books have also been consulted and the more important of these are listed below

*A Survey of the City of Worcester.*1764. Valentine Green.

The History and Antiquities of the City and Suburbs of Worcester. 1796.Valentine Green.

Worcester Pottery and Porcelain 1751-1851. 1877. R.W.Binns.

Worcester China, a record of the work of forty five years 1852-1897. 1897. R.W.Binns.

Coloured Worcester Porcelain of the First Period (1751-1783). 1954. Henry Rissik Marshall. Includes full account of the process of making china at Warmstry manufactory as detailed in booklet published in 1810 (see page 8).

The Illustrated Guide to Worcester Porcelain. 1751-1793. 1969. Henry Sandon.

Worcester Porcelain. 1950.Dr. F.Severne Mackenna (see page 9).

Flight and Barr Worcester Porcelain 1783-1840. 1978. Henry Sandon. Includes interesting extracts from the diary of John Flight and the Account Books of James Ross.

Chamberlain-Worcester Porcelain 1788-1852. 1982. Geoffrey A. Godden FRSA. Includes the full article, *A Day at the Royal Porcelain-works, Worcester (The Penny Magazine,* February 1843). Also has details of Chamberlain artists, modellers and gilders.

Grainger's Worcester Porcelain. 1989. Henry and John Sandon. Includes details of the factory workforce.

Royal Worcester Porcelain from 1862 to the Present Day. 1973. Henry Sandon. Includes much information on employees and also has interesting extracts from the diary of Henry Baldwyn.